# Dorm Delights

# IS $20 a week enough to feed a hungry student? Why, yes of course!

Are you a broke college student with no money? Yet you still want to eat 5 star delicious meals, just like when you were living at home? Then this cookbook is right for you!

Like every college student out there, I have also struggled to keep my beer budget high and my food budget low. But now, after having been in College for 5 years, I have equipped myself with all of the amazing money saving tricks one can do with food, in order to ensure delicious meals everyday at an incredibly affordable price.

More than a cookbook, this book provides the template and lifestyle required to maintain such a low food budget. Not only are these recipes cheap, they are also good for your health!

Therefore, with no further ado,
LET'S START COOKING!
REX ELARDO, CREATOR OF DRD

# YOU CAN FIND REX'S CRAZY CREATIONS ON INSTAGRAM @REX_IN_THECITY

**Introduction:**

This book is meant for college students, or other busy people, who are super duper broke but still want to go home and have a nice 5-star meal every day. As a college student myself, my food budget has been 20 dollars a week for more than four full years now. This, however, did not cover every meal. As a college student, I participated in a lot of different clubs and organizations, many of which served free food once a week. Tuesday night is Entrepreneurs club, always free pizza; Friday is Shabbat, free dinner guaranteed at the Hillel or Chabad on campus. This brings me to my first point:

**Be informed about campus events; join some clubs**

Seriously, this is the easiest way to get free food and *stay* full. Universities constantly invite speakers during lunchtime, and sometimes need to offer a free lunch to their students in order to get a high rate of attendance. Various clubs and organizations usually serve food along with whatever they are doing: the Chinese Student Association, the Real Estate Club, the Entrepreneurs Club, the Arab Student Association, NASO (Northeastern African Student Organization) and of course, my favorite places for free food events, Hillel and Chabad. So, find out which clubs, organizations and student groups are throwing free food on your campus, attend those events, and get free food! You might even learn something cool in the process while you are attending these events :). On my campus, there was an app called FeedShare, which actually updated me when free food events were happening on campus, or when there was leftover food from an event. Check to see if your college campus has a similar app; if there isn't, then it may be a good idea to create one! Group chats work as well! I was also in a group chat created by the campus events coordinator, who kept everyone updated on all events happening on campus - food related or not. Everyone in the group just shares where there is free food on campus, and indeed that is a great way to make sure to never miss an occasion for free food on your campus.

Another great club is the Community Garden Club on your college campus (or the equivalent to this club on your campus). They usually grow different herbs and vegetables according to the season. Not only is it fun watching the plants grow, but you can eat those plants after! Depending on the size of the community garden at your school, you may have lots of herbs and veggies to bring home, or just a few. No matter what, you don't even need to participate that much, you just need everyone in the club to know that you are always starving and seriously don't know where your next meal will be coming from. Which brings me to my next point:

## Inform your friends and community that you are broke

Just inform your community that you are very broke, and struggle finding where your next meal will be coming from: you will be surprised how many members of the community will reach out and try to help you. Once I was on campus, very hungry around lunch time, but there was no free lunch on campus. I was about to go buy a $1.05 cup of noodles when I ran into my friend's girlfriend, and she asked me why I was buying that. I said I was broke and hungry, and she felt so bad that she bought me a whole meal! If you are an awesome person, and you are broke, don't worry - many people have guest swipes at the dining hall that they weren't going to use anyway.
Tell your friends and everyone you know that you would love to come over some night and make dinner

for everybody: everyone thinks you are awesome, plus you get a free dinner out of it! This is especially good for a date: I routinely asked the girl to get some ingredients, and then I would teach her how to make a 5-star home cooked meal at her place. The recipes in this book are cheap, so she usually won't mind dropping a couple of bucks. Be sure to bring some ingredient yourself (the cheapest one), so it doesn't look like you are just taking advantage of her. For example: "I have everything for this recipe, I am just missing ingredients XYZ. Could you please bring some?". Another great idea is if you try to sell yourself as a personal chef. I once told this to a girl and she actually paid me ten dollars to cook for her! I got to eat that night, too. And I was probably at her place for only 40 minutes total.

I remember very well the day when my college rabbi, Mendy, asked me if I would like to bring some of his leftover food to my home on Sunday, after shabbat was over. I gladly accepted the leftovers, and that leftover ground meat and rice lasted three good meals. Which brings me to my next point:

## Do not waste anything: save your leftovers

This may sound obvious, but absolutely nothing that you buy should go to waste. That is wasted food. Wasted food = wasted money. Personally, I have also sometimes wasted food by accident because I forgot something, or bought too much of the same thing. Once, I got eight chinese broccoli at Haymarket for 1 dollar, and honestly forgot to preserve the last two or use them into a meal before they had already gone bad. But when my budget gets really tight, I make sure that everything perishable that I bought has been used or eaten. Ideally, clean your fridge once a week: you will find items that you forgot about, also see which sauces are almost empty and use them. Having a list of perishable items on your fridge is a great idea; you cross those items off as you use them, letting you know what needs to be eaten as priority. Leftovers are great: I will always remember a great chef telling me that restaurant food is just really tasty leftovers, reheated in a fancy way. He gave me the example of simple spaghetti at a restaurant: it is usually pre-cooked and then reheated with the appropriate sauce at the time of serving. Letting the spaghetti sit there, slightly cooked, allows the noodles to absorb all of the tasty juices and oils surrounding it. So, what I am trying to say is that some leftover foods taste better. Some, not all; of course a steak will taste better fresh, when it is not leftover steak. But, more importantly, you can transform your leftovers into a completely different dish. A great example of this would be for my leftover ground meat tacos (pg 15).

When finishing any food placed in a container, keep the jars, you can use them later as storage. Keep as many containers as you can actually, they can all be turned into good use after being washed. When overused, discard them. Get your money's worth out of everything. And out of everywhere you go as well. This means keeping track of all food you have on hand. Which brings us to the next point:

**Keep track of everything in your fridge; note everything down**

This may sound like a no-brainer, but a lot of people actually forget this crucial step: keep track of every single piece of food that you have on hand. This way, nothing spoils. I cannot describe the number of times that my roommates have bought a lot of food, claiming that they will eat it all, and at least half of the food just goes to waste. Look, I get it, people get busy in college and don't have time to deal with cooking, or they just don't want to put the effort into chopping that one onion needed. However, the fresher the ingredient, the better it tastes. The more you wait, the higher the chances are for fresh food becoming spoiled. Especially when getting eight broccolis for one dollar, you will realize that broccoli gets old fast. You will also forget how much broccoli you actually have on hand. So, in order to minimize waste, have some post-its or simply a chalk or dry-erase board where you note everything in the fridge along with when it was purchased. This way, you can easily prioritize your menu: what should be eaten when, in order for nothing to spoil. General rule of thumb: fruits and vegetables rarely stay fresh for more than a week, so consider that and eat them fast!

Another important step is to always buy less at the market, not more. The more food is bought, the more chances there are that the food will not be eaten and eventually spoil. For dry goods, this is not an issue, but for fresh goods, be on the lookout! It is better going to the supermarket three times a week and finishing your supply of food bought each time, instead of shopping everything at once, just to realize down the line that some of the stuff bought was unnecessary. Plus, the more often you go, you will be falling on more interesting daily deals which pop up at the grocery store! Whatever you can't finish, be sure to preserve it. Which is my next point:

**Store/preserve all and any ingredients which are about to go bad**

There is not a single ingredient on this planet which cannot be preserved. Beef that is about to go bad can be cured and/or transformed into jerky, or at the very least frozen. Fresh herbs that are about to go bad can be dried. Onions that are about to go bad can be fried to become crispy onion chips, a classic Chinese noodle topping. Cucumbers and other vegetables can be pickled. The only ingredient which can actually go bad are dairy items, like cheese and milk. To avoid this, you can cook the cheese and make cheese crisps (which are absolutely delicious and incredibly simple, extending the shelf life of the cheese a bit) or you just eat the cheese before it expires. For milk, make cheese out of the milk! Or make condensed milk, which is incredible when homemade. Basically, look up how to preserve whatever ingredient on the internet and I can almost guarantee that some creative person has thought of a great way to keep the ingredient useable for longer. Whether it be vegetables, meat, herbs, tea or even marijuana, there are ways to keep that stuff fresh or alive for longer. I have never had to waste fish, just because I like fish so much and eat it almost immediately after I buy it. Also, because fish is expensive, I know where my fish is at all times. Regardless, the combo of keeping updated with all ingredients + preserving the ones that don't make it will ensure that you are getting the biggest bang out of every buck spent.

### Get the free stuff they offer at fast food places and restaurants

Some condiments never need to be bought at the store. Technically, you never need to buy salt, pepper or sugar. There are some stores that give that to you for free. I never bought ketchup in college, not once. That's because whenever I wanted ketchup I would go to the Popeyes in the Curry Student Center food court and just take a bunch of ketchup packets. Same goes with that sweet pickle relish or Cholula hot sauce. Just fill up a couple of those ramekins with hot sauce, that will last you a couple of servings!

Most bakeries throw away a lot of food. They just stick a trash bag full of bread that was unsold that day and leave it next to the trash can. The bread needs to be baked fresh every day at most bakeries, but it does not mean that the bread that was thrown out at night is inedible! It is just not tasty enough for the customer. Same goes with many pre-made sandwiches that don't get eaten the day they were made. So, make friends with everyone who works in big food chains, like Panera for example: they always have leftover food at the end of the day. If you go dumpster diving there about one hour after they close you are almost guaranteed to fall on some bags full of stale bread. Many things can be done with stale bread: you can toast it, make breadcrumbs with it, use it to thicken soups, make some bread puddings, French Toast... possibilities with stale bread are almost endless.

A great example I have is with a very good friend of mine who works at Cafe Nero (hi Katie!). Whenever I would invite her over to my place after she came from work, she always brought leftover sandwiches to give out. Sure, the bread was stale, but the ingredients were still fresh from that day. You warm up the bread, ideally in a panini press, but no matter what, deconstructing the sandwich, toasting the bread and putting the sandwich back together tastes very good as well. My point is: make as many friends as you can who work in the food industry! They tend to have a lot of free food to give out.

When you go to the dining hall, be sure to bring a bag or a tupperware with you. There will always be some food that stores pretty well which you can take with you. I usually took the bagels and the cookies in my bag. But every dining hall is different; maybe in another dining hall the fruit salad remains tasty three days after the day it is served; it depends on the dining hall. What is certain is, every dining hall has its specialty. Get to know the ins and outs of your dining hall, as well as the dining hall hacks. I used to love making pizza sandwiches, until I realised one day that using the panini press (waffle iron because my dining hall did not have a panini press) on the vegan pizza is what tastes best for a pizza panini. As usual, experiment, taste, and see what you like and what you don't like. No matter what, it will be a fun experience. But wait, when are we actually buying food? The food budget is not 0 dollars a week after all…

**When actually buying the food**
Check out which farmers markets are cheapest. In Boston, it's Haymarket, as they sell produce that is

considered too "ugly" for restaurants. Go to the market one or two hours before all of the stands close, on its last day of the week. The farmers who are at the market will be heading home that night, and whatever they don't sell will absolutely go to waste. So late, that they don't mind giving eight cucumbers for $1, or even a whole box of eggplants for $2. Sometimes they just give more than they advertise, like when this one guy said five oranges for $1, but ended up giving me ten because he didn't want his oranges going to waste!

For staples, such as rice and pasta, you have to buy in bulk if you're trying to stay cheap. Costco is ideal, but if you're in a city, honestly the large Asian markets usually have surprisingly good deals on rice. You will be eating a lot of this, so a better quality rice for three dollars more is usually well worth it in the long run. Check Amazon or Ebay for good bulk deals as well, those can be nice because they ship directly to your home for free most of the time.

I am aware that a 40 or 50 lb bag of rice may be a bit over $20 (like $22-28), so indeed there may be a week where you need to increase your weekly budget a bit. However, that bag of rice will probably last you a month or two, if not more! The standard for me was a 40lb bag of rice usually took about one full semester to finish, so yes I had to decrease my budget from $20 dollars a week to $16 or $15 for the next couple of weeks, but that was fine because I had so much rice at home which I could use in case I was hungry. If super tight on cash, split the cost of the bag of rice with your roommates or friends. You can also just sell some of your rice to floormates or other people for a profit, and may even be able to break even before using up less than half of the bag of rice. Some people don't mind paying a buck or two for a pound of rice, saving the hassle of going to the grocery store, trust me :)

Basically, my point is, when living on the cheap like this, buying in bulk is the smartest way to save money in the long run. Just make sure that you are not eating more just because you have more non-perishable food laying around the house, that's all.

Usually, the bulk of your purchases will be the 1st couple of days in the dorm. You have to buy the rice, the sauces, and the cookware. Once that is out of the way, the budget can be stable again. But, as mentioned before, you can choose to decrease your budget by a couple of dollars for the remaining month or two in order to compensate. Honestly, if you have the bulk nonperishable goods, thanks to places like Haymarket, some weeks can really be as cheap as 10 dollars… you will never grow hungry either!

Do NOT go shopping at a convenience store, ever! Convenience stores, especially the ones on a college campus, are ridiculously overpriced. You can buy one onion for $1.50 at the convenience store, but you can buy a 40lb bag of onions for $3 at the farmers market! (Haymarket for me). I know these stores are convenient, but we are in the saving money business, so we have to make that extra amount of effort to stay cheap.

Finally, make sure to network, A LOT. You honestly never know when your next free meal will come from, but the more people you know, the more chances they will invite you to events with free food. Make sure all of your friends know that you are a great cook, and are more than willing to come to their place and help them cook some nights. That's more free food which can come your way. At fancy parties, there are always nice snacks to nibble on. You make it a big snack, that's a decently sized meal right there. Mozzarella sticks and chicken skewers for dinner? Sounds awesome!

## Have a backup super cheap meal, for emergency purposes

Sometimes, there is no free lunch or dinner on campus, nobody in your community has food to give, and you are on campus, far from home, hungry. During these types of situations, you will probably have no choice but to buy food on campus (unless you brought a couple of snacks with you from home). This is why it is very important to know where the absolute cheapest and most filling meal is on your campus. It should never be more than $1.50, and should be just enough food to last you until you get home or until the next free food event. On my campus, the options were a toasted bagel with cheese, a cup of noodles, or a peanut butter and jelly sandwich with the employee discount that I get when my friend is working at the food court (he always gives me that employee discount when he works there). Not amazing food, but it will keep you full until you can get better food later on in the day. So, find those hidden gems on campus! Especially during finals week when you will most likely live in the library, knowing this information will come in handy! Where can I find the cheapest food possible, in case of an emergency?

**Getting cookware**

Honestly, my book is not about this, as this part is not, and cannot be, included in my 20 dollar a week food budget. But the best piece of advice I can give about this is for you to buy those all-in-one sets on the internet. I bought mine on eBay, but you can also find them on Amazon. For 100-150 dollars, you can get spoons, bowls, knives, pans, one baking tray and some pots. Just make sure you choose a set which favors quality, instead of one set which gives like four different sized pots and five different sized pans. You only really need one good pot and one good pan for all of your cooking. All I am saying is, quality is better than quantity for these sets!

Also, check if any friends or family are willing to donate some cookware to you. That's where most of my cookware comes from, actually. Also, sometimes there are programs like "trash to treasure" at universities which sell whatever college students left inside their dorm from the previous semester for extremely cheap. I got a perfectly functional rice cooker for $5 thanks to one of these programs. Many good things come out of this, so it is definitely worth it in my opinion!

However, just to be clear: you don't need that many materials to cook. If you have a knife, spoon, fork, pot and a pan, you can make basically everything there is out there. Maybe a mixing bowl and baking tray are nice as well, but you can always mix inside the pot and bake inside the pan if low on kitchen utensils. A fork can replace a whisk and is also a very good meat pounder/tenderizer.

So, if you are in a dorm, get the cheap set because you know you will throw it out after, and you can damage the crap out of your kitchen utensils without really caring.

However, if you know that you will be sticking around the house for a while, it might make sense to buy a $20 pot that will last 20 years, instead of buying $5 pots over and over that only last two years. The most important thing, however, is to have at least some utensils, regardless whether they are good or not. Without utensils, it is a lot tougher to cook!

**#1 point of this book**:

Have fun! Try something new! if it doesn't taste good the first time, do not give up! I have failed making every recipe countless times before I found the right balance in flavor and ingredients for each dish. Just remember that cooking is meant to be fun, so relax and and enjoy every recipe this book provides you with!

**Disclaimer:**

For every single recipe posted, just know that it is ok if the recipe is not followed to the letter. There is a reason why I do not say how much of each ingredient needs to be put into the dish. Cooking is not an exact science. I will hint at how much is needed (a pinch, a handful), but I want everyone using this cookbook to get into the habit of never needing to measure any of their ingredients, and to just start eyeballing the correct amount. This is what every seasoned chef does! Unless he is baking, which is definitely more of a science.

I understand that most people reading this have a limited budget and may only be able to buy the discounted veggies every week, which tend to vary day by day. Sometimes the cheapest veggie is okra,

while other days it's collard greens; you never know what life brings along. If my recipe calls for broccoli and all you have is Chinese broccoli, zucchini or some other vegetable similar to broccoli (cauliflower maybe?), then use that instead, it will probably still taste great. Just make sure you are taking into account the textural consideration when doing this: broccoli is very crunchy, whereas zucchini is a softer kind of vegetable. No matter what, after trial and error you may accidentally come up with great combinations that might be even better than the recipes in the book! I am just giving a simple template, as well as ideas for how to build on that template. You can do whatever you want with these recipes. You can omit an ingredient or two, and see if it still tastes ok.
True fact: you can replace cheese with salt (some people like adding nutritional yeast as well, easy to get a couple of servings for free at any Whole Foods). The dish may be less cheesy, but it will definitely still have a lot of flavor. SO, if one of my recipes calls for cheese and you don't have any because it is the end of the week and your budget is running too low, then don't use the cheese. Unless of course the main ingredient of the dish is cheese, like grilled cheese for example. Omit the cheese, you basically just get toasted bread.

A great example of this ingredient omission is one day when I wanted to make mac and cheese(main ingredient is mac here, not cheese!), but unfortunately did not have the money for cheese. I did have stale bread however, and some herbs (I believe Parsley). So I toasted the bread, crushed it up to make breadcrumbs, toasted those breadcrumbs again (making the breadcrumbs extra crunchy), added some herbs (parsley and basil), a little bit of spice like chili flakes, and then added cooked pasta to these breadcrumbs while they were toasting. The result was incredible; I fell in love with breadcrumb pasta. All I am trying to say with this example is that even without every ingredient, use a bit of creativity and you will be able to achieve greatness of flavor.

Once I was so poor I didn't even have money for breadcrumbs. No bread in the house, just flour. So I made the breadcrumb pasta recipe replacing the breadcrumbs with flour: I seasoned the flour with herbs and spices, toasted it with a little bit of water to get a nice golden brown color, and then added pasta to that. Honestly, the result was pretty good. Of course real breadcrumbs may have been better suited for breadcrumb pasta, but I definitely preferred eating the flour substitute for breadcrumb pasta than eating just plain pasta with some herbs on it.

I will do my best in this book to help you get as many ideas as possible. I will add at least a couple of substitutes for some ingredients for each and every one of my recipes, but even with that there may be times when that is still not enough. That is when I advise, even recommend, that you be creative with your options. When living this much down the line (20 dollars a week! I still have no idea how I survived college with this budget), just remember that there will definitely be times with ingredients missing. It will not taste as optimal as it should, but it will still taste good and you will feel full after. That's what really matters.

So, after reading my disclaimer, just understand that you should take every recipe with a grain of salt! (haha get it?) I am trying to make high end cooking and the most delicious dishes possible with only 20 dollars a week; this means that no matter what, in many occasions, I absolutely need to be using every cheap trick there is in the book. When dealing with such few ingredients, execution is key to making it taste incredible, like if it were at a 5 star restaurant. How is it that something as simple as roasted potatoes (literally one tbsp of oil and potatoes + salt and some herbs, if you want) can be so good? You have to make sure everything is executed perfectly. Check the potatoes five minutes before the recipe says to; maybe your oven runs very hot. Some ovens take five minutes longer. Make sure all potatoes are roughly the same size. When the execution is perfect, the food will taste perfect as well.

**What NOT to do:**

This may sound simple, but I seriously mean it: DO NOT EAT OUT! Unless you are getting 1 dollar slices of pizza or are not counting this into your food budget, just don't do it! This will absolutely destroy your food budget. One sandwich is 7 dollars on average; how can I eat for the next 5 meals if I do this? No more Starbucks or fancy hipster coffee shops, either. I got 100 bags of green tea from the Asian supermarket (Super 8 in Packards Corner) for $4, and still have a lot of bags left 6 months later. I am also usually present at the "Hora del Cafe" which happens at the Latino student center every Wednesday, which hands out free tea and coffee; they definitely did not mind when I started shoving multiple bags of tea down my pocket, they understood my broke financial situation. Be sure to reuse bags of tea in order to get the most optimal value out of your purchase!.

If you absolutely NEED coffee, then make it at home and use a French press. Coffee filters may be cheap but the cost does rack up. No matter what, no more coffee at Starbucks or other coffee shops, those places just eat your money and you are not even full after. Not worth it, just don't do it! If you can't get away from it, then just know that it cannot count towards your food budget. Food budget = food. You can drink water. Everything else budget = everything else. This includes beer!

Unless you decrease your food budget, because you want to remain at 20 dollars a week total budget (this is tough), remember that all you can buy with these 20 dollars every week is food. Just remember, as a disclaimer.

**Reminder/ credits/ special thanks**

As long as you are having fun, please, continue cooking! If you fail a dish or two, it's ok! You will succeed next time! I will admit that I failed many recipes before I came up with the cheapest and greatest recipes found below, which is why I must give a huge shoutout to all of the people in college who made sure I didn't starve to death. Huge thanks to Jerry, Bruno, Dario, Aaron, Josh, Arivu, Paige, Joaquin, and of course, Mohamed. I would have gone hungry more than once throughout college if it wasn't thanks to you guys!

**Before the recipes: small preserving tips**

A big part of this cookbook is to not waste anything that you buy. When things are on the verge of going bad, there are many ways to "save" the ingredients, or so to speak. These preserving tips will make sure that the least amount of food is wasted:

- Preserving herbs: dry them in the oven! At low heats, the oven can dry the herbs, allowing a longer shelf life. You can also put

the herbs into some oil in order to make some beautiful aromatic herb oil
- Vegetables: pickle them! Carrots, turnip, cucumber… any vegetable is a great candidate for pickling, except for potato maybe
- Bread: make breadcrumbs! Just keep the stale bread, as wonders can be made from it, trust me. French toast is also a very good option for stale bread, of course
- Rice: fry it! Fried rice the next day is always delicious, nobody says no to that idea. Rice soup is also another viable option, as well as a rice porridge-type thing
- Beans: preserve the cooking liquid! There are a million different things we can do with that: sauce or dip thickener, soup base, flavored water, just to name a few
- Meat and fish: cure it! Or eat it while it is still fresh. Not all meats and fish are good for curing, but most definitely are, and with a little bit of salt and spices, magic can happen for sure
- Food scraps: they can still be used for stock! So don't throw them out just yet
- Stock: freeze it! If you are making homemade stock, make a lot in order to have some leftover after, which can be used at any time, as long as you freeze it or store it properly.

This is when all of the food scraps I mentioned before become extremely useful
- Fruit: ferment it! I will agree that some fruits can go bad, so how about fermenting them and retrieving their probiotic properties? It's fun to mess with this, but sometimes you definitely end up with funky flavors, so be careful. If you know the art of fermentation, try to ferment anything that is about to go bad. Youtube actually taught me all of the tricks needed for fermentation. Fruit salad is also an incredibly good idea, or you can boil the fruit and extract its juice if there is just too much fruit. Making jam is also possible
- Smoke: you can smoke some foods, like fish or meat or vegetables, to preserve them if you have access to a smoker (probably very rare). homemade oven smokers are a thing though

**Flavored waters**

Have you noticed that at most spas and cafeterias they have cucumber water, and that stuff is totally refreshing and delicious? So, why not have some of that refreshing drink at home at all times? your friends will think that you live in a fancy spa or something!

Do you know why all of these spas give out this fancy water as if it were nothing? it's because making flavored water is ridiculously cheap! This is definitely one of those tricks that will impress your guests, they will think they are drinking some crazy craft hipster drink even though in reality it is incredibly cheap to make. The recipe:

Flavored water:
- Water
- Anything you want to soak into the water (I recommend using fruit scraps, they can get the water quite tasty)

Fill a jug with water. add to this jug the items you want to soak into the water. Let sit in the fridge for at least one day, and no more than a couple of weeks. you can refill the jug with water multiple times, if you would like. I once made more than 20 strawberry water bottles using the same initial strawberries, and the water was still not bland!

Flavored water ideas (can always use only one instead of both):
- Cucumber and mint water
- Lemon lime water
- Strawberry kiwi water
- Basil and fennel water
- Orange and cherry water
- Ginger and lemon water
- Tea and ginger water

Just to name a few. Be sure to use creativity and come up with your own crazy concoctions!

RECIPES

**Pickling anything**

Pickles, pickles, pickles… everybody loves pickles! They add that bright acidity that you need for your dish. Not only are they cheap in the supermarket, they are even cheaper when you make them at home! Best part, you can pickle almost anything! I have picked onions, carrots, apples, pears, cabbage, cucumbers (obviously), garlic, kohlrabi, celery, leeks, and many more vegetables! They usually come out amazing! Just be careful to dose the salt and sugar properly, or else your pickles won't be properly balanced.

Pickles are great sides to almost any occasion, and can be a relatively healthy snack as well. So, let's get pickling!

Pickles:
- Your pickling vegetable (onions, peppers, chilis, carrots… any food item can be pickled really)
- Some kind of acid (white vinegar highly recommended, but technically you can pickle with any acid - once I used lime juice and it added a nice tang to the pickle)
- Water
- Salt

- Sugar (optional, really depends if you want a sweet pickle or not)
- Pickling herbs and spices (as desired - some people put none (for a clean, crisp taste), some add dill, some add basil, peppercorn, salt, onions…)
- A jar

Mix the water, salt, acid, sugar (optional). You want the salinity to be around 2-5% (10% for olives), so do the math and don't go too crazy on the salt and the sugar. You are definitely adding less salt into the water than when cooking pasta. Bring the pickling brine to a boil. Put the pickling vegetables into the jar, with the pickling herbs and spices if desired. Pour the still boiling liquid into the jar with the pickling vegetables. Make sure every vegetable is completely covered in liquid, or it will rot. Seal the lid after it has cooled down enough, and store in the fridge. Done! Wait a couple of hours, and that's it! Mmmh, any time of the day is a good time for a nice crunchy pickle, I must say.

**The ultimate grilled cheese sandwich**

Making a grilled cheese sandwich is not hard. Making a GOOD grilled cheese sandwich is a lot harder. There are not too many ingredients involved in a grilled cheese sandwich, but it is always possible to add extra layers inside, making it a fuller and more complete meal.

I will show how to make the basics of a grilled cheese sandwich, and then give some recommendations on what could be added to the grilled cheese sandwich, as well as a killer tomato soup to accompany the sandwich, if you are so inclined to make it. Of course, any canned tomato soup will do the trick, but making your own soup in big batches can be cheaper than cans. Tomato soup keeps for a while when placed in tupperware, and also still tastes great after being frozen. It can always be used as a base for different soups and/or sauces. For toppings, add some cream, a dash of vodka (optional), some basil (expensive but worth it), touch of black pepper, and there you go! A killer creamy tomato soup!

## TOMATO SOUP:
The best tomato soup is created with pure simplicity. if you have the luck of falling on a can of San Marzano tomatoes, those are some of the best tomatoes in the world to be made into tomato sauce or soup. Just so much real tomato flavor in there. If not, no worries, this is dorm room cooking after all. This is dorm cooking, after all; any can of peeled tomatoes will do the trick.

- Can of peeled tomatoes (or fresh tomatoes which you peel yourself)
- Water
- Onions
- Herbs (ideally bay leaf and basil, but if too expensive parsley will add herb flavoring)
- One garlic clove, diced/pressed
- Oil (herb oil or chili oil works incredibly well. Classic would be olive oil, of course)
- Teeny bit of butter (around 1/2tbsp, can be replaced by oil)
- Salt

OPTIONAL ITEMS
- Splash of white wine
- Carrots
- Celery
- Whole spicy peppers, grilled or charred for smoky flavor if desired

TOPPINGS (all optional)
- Dash of heavy cream (ideally creme fraiche. Sour cream works fine too)
- Dash of vodka
- Bit of olive oil
- Toasted nuts and/or seeds (ideally not peanuts; my favorite for this recipe are sunflower seeds)
- Basil
- Black pepper

Heat up pot, medium heat. Add oil (or butter) to pan. Add onions and garlic (plus optional carrots and celery), until onions are translucent. Add white wine to deglaze the pan (optional), then add tomatoes and herbs (except basil, that goes at the end). simmer for 10-30 minutes, or until consistency is thick. Simmer more or less depending on how thick you want your soup. If adding bay leaves, remove them from the pot once desired thickness is reached. Blend the pot mixture in a blender. Thicken the soup with that little knob of butter. Season with salt. Finish with toppings (optional) and basil (or any other chopped herb laying around. better to have some finishing herb that adds a slight kick than no herb at all. Oregano, parsley, thyme or rosemary can all work exceptionally well).
EAT THE TOMATO SOUP. Delicious, right?
PS: if serving with grilled cheese, it is best to make the tomato soup a bit thicker, so that it is even more satisfying to dip the grilled cheese sandwich in the soup. So just leave on the stove a bit longer before adding the butter, thickening it up more.
HOW TO MAKE KOSHER: it already is kosher! Just don't finish with cheese and replace the butter with margarine if serving meat.
ADD BACON: yes, some rendered crispy bacon can finish the dish quite nicely! The best kosher alternative to that is beef fry, although expensive it sure is tasty :)

TOMATO SAUCE:
If cooked down enough, this tomato soup can actually become tomato sauce! Just cook it down for longer, at a lower temperature, and don't add any of the final toppings (except for basil, if you like).

## GRILLED CHEESE SANDWICH

This is seriously one of the most simple and amazing dishes that exist on the face of this earth. So, ideally you have the usual texas toast bread and awesome cheddar cheese, but don't be afraid to get creative and use other breads and cheeses! This is dorm cooking: any bread combined with any cheese will technically work, and be absolutely delicious :)

Grilled cheese:
- Bread
- Cheese
- Mayonnaise (can be replaced by butter, but butter is expensive and mayo works just fine. If super duper poor, make your own mayo, page xx)
- Pinch of salt, pepper

Heat up pan. While waiting, put cheese between two slices of bread. Spread the outside with mayonnaise. Toast sammich in pan on medium heat. Flip once;

once cheese is oozing, it is ready! Make sure that the exterior is nice and golden brown. Add salt and pepper to your own liking.

Fancy additional stuff you can put in the sandwich:
- Onions
- Grilled mushrooms
- Spinach
- Tomatoes
- Garlic (preferably fried)
- Meats
- Peppers (hot or not; grilled is also very nice)
- Herbs (basil, thyme are my favorite)

SUPER fancy addition/ trick:
Cover the outside with parmesan cheese. It makes the outside golden brown, cheesier, and more parmesan-ey. Nothing could be better, but of course parmesan is expensive so this is optional, but great when you are trying to impress your guests with a gourmet grilled cheese!

## Making your own mayo

Mayo is incredibly simple to make! It just requires a lot of whisking, and a lot of patience. Technically, one egg yolk is enough to make a whole jar of mayo! Be sure to add the oil gradually, ensuring that it the mayo does not break. If you do break your mayo, you will need another egg yolk and gradually add the broken mayo to that. A mayo is an emulsion after all, so it is very delicate. Be sure to not break the mayo!

Mayo:
- Egg yolk (keep the egg whites, you can use them for egg white omelettes or meringues or many other things)
- Oil (neutral oil for normal mayo, herb oil for herb mayo, olive oil for olive oil mayo etc)
- Mustard (or lemon juice, or even water technically)
- Acid (optional; white vinegar and lemon juice work best, as they are neutral acids)
- A couple of pinches of salt

Whisk the egg yolk with the mustard (or substitute), salt, and acid, adding oil slowly while still whisking. Eventually, the mixture will thicken and turn into mayo. Just make sure to not pour the oil too quickly, or the mayo will 'break' and you will need another egg yolk to fix the problem. Add the broken mayo to the egg yolk slowly, as if it were oil.

Making mayo is definitely easier in a food processor or electric mixer, but if you have enough willpower you can make mayo using only a fork or a whisk. In that case, more effort is needed to make the mayo is all.

Enjoy the mayo, and use it as you would normal mayo! It has up to one month shelf life as long as it is inserted in a sealed container and refrigerated.

**Leftover tacos**

Tacos are the best. Everybody loves tacos: they are just corn tortillas filled with stuff in the middle. Most leftovers can be turned into tacos: my rule of thumb is that as long as it is placed on top of a corn tortilla, then it is good enough to be a taco. Just make sure to add the triad of mexican ingredients into the taco, in order to make it taste mexican enough. I made my mexican leftover tacos with some leftover ground beef (cooked burger patties or hotdogs work just as well) but feel free to add any sorts of leftovers, there is no limit! Tofu, greens, cabbage... the imagination and possibilities are limitless!

LEFTOVER BEEF TACO:
*The mexican triad:*
-Garlic, minced
-Lime
-Salt
-Cumin (optional)
-Cilantro, shredded (optional)
-Spice (optional, ideally jalapenos or habaneros). Can be charred (blackened) for extra smoky flavor.

*The taco filling:*
-Leftover ground beef
-Onions, julienned
-Bell peppers
-Mexican triad
-Corn tortillas

*The slaw (optional garnish; just mix all ingredients together in a bowl):*
-Cabbage, red and/or white, shredded
-Mayo
-Lime juice
-Garlic
-Red onion, minced (optional)
-Salt
-Pepper
-Cilantro, chopped (optional)
-Touch of cumin (optional)


Put the garlic, onions and peppers (optional) in pan, medium high heat. Heat until golden brown. Add meat, and brown it a little bit more. Add the mexican triad to the mix. Set aside.
Heat up the tortillas on the pan that was used to make the taco filling. This way the tortillas soak up all of those leftover pan juices, yummmm.

Finally, fill tortilla with filling. Squeeze some lime on top, as garnish. You can also garnish with chopped cabbage, as well as minced cilantro and onion. The slaw recipe above is also a great garnish, making it a little bit more of a California-style taco. If you are rich enough, the best topping in the world for tacos must be Queso Fresco. However, if using cheese you must replace that leftover beef with veggie meat in order to keep the dish kosher! Should be amazing regardless, kosher or not :)

**Matzo ball soup**

This dish is one of my favorite soups ever. It is so heartwarming, feels so homey. My grandmother never used to make me matzo ball soup, but many of my friends' grandmothers definitely know how to make some good matzo ball soup!

Matzo ball soup:
- Veggie (or beef) stock (or you can make your own stock, learn page xxx)
- Onions, chopped roughly
- Carrot, chopped roughly
- Matzo meal (can be replaced by any type of bread-breadcrumb-starch based substance)
- Celery(optional)
- Croutons (optional; the classic crouton is the 'mandel' type crouton)

- Oil (or chicken fat, or any cool type of fat if you have. Duck fat is really delicious)
- Egg
- Herbs, spices (optional; traditionally only dill is necessary at the end, as a topping)

Warm broth. Peel and roughly chop the carrots and onion. Stick them inside the hot stock, until they are very soft.

While waiting, make matzo balls. Mix oil, egg and matzo meal until you can form balls. For one cup of matzo meal, two eggs are needed. Feel free to add herbs and spices to this mix. Add a bit of salt. Make proper sized dumplings, the ideal size in my opinion being about the size of a golf ball. Add dumplings to soup. lower heat. Once matzo balls are nice and soggy, floating to the surface, the soup is ready. Finish with garnish and croutons. A famous garnish is dill, as it really gives a nice fresh final touch to the dish.

What is fun about matzo ball soup is that you can fill the dumpling with anything you want! Meat, veggie puree (page xxx), or even some herbs! But don't worry, the classic matzo ball has no filling in it whatsoever! So, if you want authenticity, then definitely do not fill your matzo ball, leave it the way it is! You can also try replacing the oil for some melted butter (or margarine if you are serving meat after and want to keep kosher), if you can afford it.

The classic crouton is that israeli brand that my local rabbi always uses (the 'mandel') but any crouton is better than no crouton if 'mandel' is too hard to find. I like my croutons extra crunchy, so sometimes dry or stale bread can be re-fried in a pan and then used as the ultimate crouton.

**Cheese sticks**

These are the best snacks that money can buy. It is basically just flour, butter and cheese, but doesn't that sound absolutely delicious? I am seriously addicted to these things. Make sure to split the cost of the dish with your roommates, especially if they start eating all of the sticks you worked so hard to create. The recipe:

Cheese sticks:
- Flour
- Butter
- Egg
- Cheese, shredded (ideally cheddar cheese, but any cheese will work, even mozzarella)
- Salt, pepper

Mix the flour and the butter, until formation of a crumbly dough. Add the cheese, then the egg, salt, and pepper, until a ball forms. Roll out the dough and cut into 1 inch, pinky-size thick sticks. Bake them on a tray lined with parchment paper in the oven, for around 20 minutes on 210C (400F) until they are golden brown. The amazing cheese sticks are now officially ready! Sprinkle with salt and pepper. Great on their own, or when dunked into many different dipping sauces :)

## Veggie puree

Ah, this is a great way to make use of copious amounts of veggies. By blending all of the veggies together, adding some oil (butter ideally) at the end, you end up with this unctuous puree, which is a great side for all types of dishes, from other grilled veggies to chicken to tofu to fish and so on. The concept of veggie puree is so simple! Feel free to try different combinations of veggies, and see which combinations you prefer the most. I will try to keep the recipe as simple as possible, and let your imagination grow free with this veggie puree.

*Veggie puree:*
- Veggies
- Salt, pepper
- Stock (optional, can replace with water)
- Butter (ideal but optional and can be replaced by oil if truly necessary)

- Seasonings (my favorite for most veggies tend to be some garlic, minced with ginger, and one bunch of parsley)
- Creme fraiche (optional)

Boil/broil/bake/grill your veggies. I don't care how you do it, try different methods and see which one works best for which vegetable. I will supply some classic veggie puree preparations and examples at the end of this recipe, of course.

Once the veggies are soft and mashable, stick those veggies in the blender with some stock (water if you don't have or if you want to preserve the pure veggie flavor), butter (or oil) and seasonings. Blend until the smoothest paste possible comes out. If you don't have a blender, then just mash it with a masher (or just a fork will work), until it becomes a puree. It may be a bit more rustic looking, but will still be just as delicious. Season with salt and pepper at the end. Top each with some creme fraiche (optional) alongside a little bit of pepper, and serve.

Classic puree vegetables:
Carrots, boiled
Kohlrabi, boiled
Squash, broiled, with a little beat of heat from a chili like a habanero or something
Turnip, boiled

Potatoes, boiled (add milk instead of stock in this case)
Fennel, boiled
Artichoke hearts, grilled
Mushrooms, pan seared
Peppers, grilled
Eggplant, grilled (add tahini and garlic before blending and you basically have baba ganoush)


**Garlic pasta:**
One of my all-time favorite college staples! I loved this dish because you can call it something fancy: 'pasta aglio e olio' which is just Italian for pasta with garlic and oil. Everyone will think that you are having a super high class meal, when in real life it's just pasta with garlic and oil! The recipe:

Pasta aglio e olio:
- Pasta
- Garlic
- Oil
- Salt, pepper
- Parsley (optional but highly recommended)
- Cheese (ideally parmesan. Again optional but highly recommended)

**Note: the seasoning at the end could be cheese, but this is an expensive ingredient so salt (or nutritional yeast) can make the dish almost just as tasty.**

Boil water. Add a good handful of salt in water. Then add the pasta.

Heat up a large pan, medium-high heat. Add oil and garlic to the pan. Cook until the garlic is fragrant and starting to brown. While this is happening, drain the pasta, making sure that you are keeping some of that precious pasta water. Then, immediately add the pasta, with some pasta water, to the pan. You can add a bit of the pasta water in the pan earlier in order to prevent the garlic from burning, if your pasta is not ready to be thrown in the pan yet. Saute for at least 2-3 minutes, in order for the pasta to absorb all of that amazing garlic oil. Chop up the parsley, as fine as you can.

Finish the pasta with some chopped parsley (highly recommended). Salt and pepper to taste, as well as cheese (optional; parmesan or pecorino is ideal but once I used mexican queso fresco and it was equally as delicious).

Serve, and be amazed at how simple yet delicious this dish truly is!

Squash pasta:
- Pasta, preferably butterfly shaped
- Squash
- Garlic
- Salt, pepper

- Cream (creme fraiche is ideal, but any cream is good. Yogurt can work, too, as a substitute)
- Cheese
- Parsley (optional)

Cube up squash, the smaller the better but minced size may be too small. Cook in pan on medium high, adding garlic and salt, until the small pieces of squash are nice and brown on the outside.

Cook pasta, and strain then drop in pan with the squash, with a little bit of the pasta water as well. Add cream and cheese, with some pepper. Finish with chopped parsley (optional)

Tada! Beautiful simple delicious fall pasta, a way to make the garlic pasta recipe pop out a little bit more.

**Garlic greens**

4 ingredients, and for some reason nobody ever gets sick of this dish!

Garlic greens:
- Greens (my favorite to use for this recipe are collard greens, but any greens will work)
- Garlic, minced
- Salt
- Lemon juice (or anything comparably sour, will always opt for lemon juice if possible; however, tried with lime juice and vinegar once, both came out pretty great)

Heat up pan on high heat. Add oil. Saute garlic until golden. Add greens. Saute until greens are wilted and browning. Add salt. Finish with a lot of lemon juice. Serve!

For extra lemony flavor, remember to add lemon juice 2-3 times throughout the cooking process. If you are broke, once at the end will do the job, but it is also nice to have more lemony cooked down essence if the means are available. You can even add lemon or lime zest, if you would like!

SPICE IT UP:A teeny bit of strong cheese, like Parmesan and the like, can be amazing. Even finishing the greens with some good ole' Cheddar adds some oomph to this dish.
SUPER FANCY: nuts. Pine nuts are my fave, but walnuts or almonds can change the direction of the dish massively. You can toast the nuts before adding them to the greens, if you desire. Add a teeny bit more salt if you are adding nuts to your greens.
IF YOU WANNA GO NEXT LEVEL: shave some truffles on top of the greens, at the end. As this is a college cookbook, you most likely will never have a chance to do this in college. But, who knows? While we're at it, use some fancy finishing salt when doing this, like Maldon salt or "fleur de sel".

**Ramen deluxe**

We all know that ramen noodles are a staple of college life: cheap, delicious and oh-so filling. There are so many different flavors and brands of ramen, too: you can have anything, from cheap to expensive, from vegetable to Chinese hot pot flavor. However, no matter which flavor you choose, packaged ramen will still be packaged ramen. It is just noodles with soup, and gets boring after a while.

Therefore, this recipe is a template for one of many ways that you can make ramen interesting again. Some of your friends will think they are eating at an actual ramen shop!

You will need:
- A packet of ramen noodles
- Some veggies --- I recommend bok Choy and chinese Broccoli for this one, but any veggie will work I promise
- Some protein (meat, fish or tofu or something -- optional)
- Some hot broth -- you can use the ramen broth packet, another broth packet if you have a favorite, but any broth, homemade or not, works! Seriously

- Some garnish (optional again, but scallions are my favorite)

This recipe is incredibly easy. Chop the ingredients into bite size pieces (minus the ramen and broth of course) then stick them into the hot boiling broth, for about 3 minutes. Once the veggies are cooked, add the noodles, turn off the heat, cover the pan and let sit for about 3 more minutes.

Voila! Dinner is served. □

My favorite veggies are pan fried enoki mushrooms, cheap and easy to cook. My favorite protein to put in is surprisingly tofu, works so well with the spicy miso broth I tend to make often. To make spicy miso broth, just combine miso paste and some spice, such as chili powder, and pour hot water over the mixture.. My favorite spice to use actually comes from a certain ramen packet, the ultra spicy one. The salty spice combined with miso paste is just awesome.

If you only have hot water and no pan, that's fine as well, this recipe can still be made. Just chop your veggies smaller and make sure they are clean veggies. Sometimes I just blanch them in a bowl of hot water for about 30 seconds before adding them to the ramen bowl. The ramen always comes out great.

No matter what, ramen will always be delicious for a college student in my book :)

## Rice balls/ cracker balls (arancini)

A fancy way to say rice ball dumplings is arancini, which is what the Italians say. Just in case you need to impress your guests.
In general, you will find that dumplings are very versatile. They can be made fancy, using expensive ingredients, but at their core dumplings have always been a poor man's food. Look at the potato knishes that used to be made in Poland, for example, or simply matzo ball soup.
The following recipe I usually make with rice, but nothing says that the rice cannot be replaced with crushed up crackers. You can even mix both of them if you want to!
I am using the ultra cheap filling method, but please feel free to customize the filling with whatever your heart wants. Putting cheese with bacon in the middle is a classic, especially if you have good mozzarella cheese which just oozes out when splitting the rice/cracker ball in half. Anyway, here is the recipe:

- Filling (example: string beans, onions, carrots, garlic, all minced. Can be replaced with boiled potatoes and peas. Just make sure you are buying the cheapest veggies at your local market. String beans can be replaced by anything green so don't worry about following

the recipe to the dot. Can add some nuts (peanuts, walnuts or other), optionally)
- Binders: flour, egg (breadcrumbs as well, if you like - optional)
- Seasonings: I like chili flakes and fresh parsley, but Basil works great. Some people like oregano a lot, especially when you serve the rice balls with tomato sauce. I like to coat the outside with breadcrumbs sometimes. Never forget the salt and pepper! If you are rich, you can add parmesan cheese to this; I have never found a single dumpling (except for Chinese dumplings) which tasted worse once parmesan was added to it. This is probably because Parmesan is like salt: it just adds seasoning and flavor to anything!
- Base: cooked rice, crackers, or even cooked Pasta should do the trick. Just make sure that all pieces are about the same size as rice would be

Make the filling: dice and cook the carrots and onions on medium heat, until the onions are translucent. Add the garlic, chopped, at the same time as the string beans. Add some nuts, any type of nut (optional). Add curry (optional).

Mix flour, egg and seasonings with the base until it is all properly mixed. Roll a ball, then make a nub in the middle with your thumb. Fill the filling into the nub of the ball, and close it. Before placing in the fryer, roll ball in seasoned flour (or seasoned breadcrumbs) once again, in order to try and make it preserve its shape.

Fry the rice/cracker ball, until golden brown. If you have enough oil to deep fry it, then that is ideal. If not, pan frying works just as great The only issue with pan frying is that the dumpling will not look like a ball anymore, it will have flat sides and look almost like a square. In that case, if pan frying I would prefer to make dumpling patties, those are equally as delicious. I highly recommend shaping the dumplings as flat patties instead of round balls when pan frying. If you are really poor, steaming these patties can work quite amazing, that's basically what a chinese Baozi is!

Again, here the filling can be anything; use a ground beef filling if you want. If you are so broke that you only have flour, no rice or pasta or crackers or breadcrumbs or anything similar, then make a dough with the seasoned flour and water, wrap the filling with some small pieces of dough, and fry that. You avoid using cooking oil this way!

If you have a little bit more money to spare, buy some puff pastry dough or phyllo dough and make samosas. They are technically dumplings as well, which can be fried or baked! You can alternatively make your own puff pastry, but it is time consuming and also requires a lot of butter. It is a rather tough dough to execute correctly. Absolutely still worth it, if you have the time for it, but as you are a busy college student maybe sticking to this recipe is best.

Enjoy your amazing appetizer! So many sauce possibilities for this too, depending on the type of dumpling you make:
- If you go Indian style (heavy spices, curry filling): chutney
- If you go Italian Style (cheese filling) : tomato sauce
- If you go Polish style (potato and peas filling): Tzatziki (recipe below) and/or just creme fraiche or sour cream with some herbs (usually dill and/or chives) is amazing.

Try different sauces and combinations, until you find your favorite: some people like Sriracha mayo on this, I disagree but hey to each their own am I right?

**Tzatziki:**
- Yogurt
- Garlic
- Lemon juice
- Cucumber
- Olive oil (optional)
- Dill (optional but recommended)
- Salt, pepper

Chop the cucumber into small pieces, as well as the garlic. Add to yogurt with salt, pepper, lemon juice, olive oil (optional) and dill (optional) to have a simple yet incredible sauce. This is great for cocktail parties, as it is the most incredible dip for crudites such as carrot or celery sticks. A lot healthier than many of the dip options out there, too!

**Garlic fried rice**

Although rice balls do taste a lot better than garlic fried rice, sometimes we are just too broke to afford more than rice, garlic and the teeniest bit of oil. Once I was so broke that I took the simple salad dressing packets from a certain store which hands them out for free (Whole Foods, shh) and separated the oil from the vinegar as best as I could. Usually you put 5-6 in a cup, then just wait a bit. The oil will float to the top, and you can use a spoon to scrape the oil from the top. You can then use the vinegar later on!

Garlic fried rice:
- Sticky Rice
- Garlic
- Oil
- Salt
- Fish flakes (optional - can also use furikake)

Make small balls with the sticky rice. Cover those balls with chopped garlic. Fry the rice balls, add some salt when golden brown and removed from fryer. Cover with fish flakes, or rice crack (called furikake). Serve. Delicious garlic rice balls! Nobody could ever ask for more :)

**Po Boy**

I must say: Louisiana has never been a rich state, and the food coming from this state is absolutely incredible, both in flavor and in cheapness. I will always remember when I went to Mardi Gras in New Orleans, and bought myself a 3 foot sandwich for less than 10 dollars. And this was at a store. Just imagine how much cheaper it can get!

I will show you how to make your own simple, cheap and delicious dough, because it is cheaper than the supermarket, but that does take time so don't feel bad if you are buying one of those large loaves of Italian bread (or other bread) for under 3 dollars. You could probably do 3 servings with a loaf of bread that big! So not bad at all.

Also, what I am filling my Po Boy with is just a suggestion; again, feel free to fill your po boy with whatever you want. It is a Po Boy as long as there are these 3 elements:
- The filling contains something fried

- The bread is a baguette-type bread (meaning it has a harder crust; no wonderbread here)
- There is a remoulade sauce

As long as there are those three elements, congrats! You have just made yourself a po boy.

My version of Po Boy has these three elements: you can fry a nicer protein, like fish or shrimp, or you can fry something a little bit less costly, probably vegetables like zucchini or squash or something. I once made an asian style po boy, making my fried filling tofu and then making the remoulade a bit more Asian tasting by adding fish sauce and a teeny bit of soy sauce and lime juice (omitting the salt). You can also add scallions to that Asian remoulade. Remember, it is always most important to have fun and experiment!

<u>The bread:</u>
The best would be a simple, baguette type bread. That is a true Po Boy. Dough needs to rise about 2 hours minimum
- Flour
- Yeast
- Water
- Salt (pinch)

- Sugar (pinch)
- Oil (tbsp)
- Herbs (optional)

Mix all dry ingredients together. Mix yeast with water. Add mixture to flour. Mix and knead until it becomes a dough. Add more flour if necessary, more water if necessary.

Knead furiously, punching the dough if you like. Once it has been kneaded for about 5 minutes, let the dough rise with a damp cloth. Let rest about 2 hours. After the 2 hours, knead the dough again for one minute, and shape the bread how you want. For Po Boy, it is better to make one big loaf of bread. Make sure to put a couple of slices around the top of the loaf, in order to make sure that no air bubbles get caught and the bread explodes!

Stick in the oven for 20-30 mins, medium high heat. Voila! You have a nice loaf of bread now, which you made all by yourself :)

The filling:

I am going to fry some chicken with some zucchini, as an example. But, as stated before, any vegetable or meat can be fried, and it will taste great! Fish can work as well

- Chicken

- Egg
- Flour
- Breadcrumbs
- Zucchini
- Spices (cajun spice is recommended, we are doing a NOLA style po boy after all)
- Onion powder (Optional)
- Garlic powder (Optional)
- Salt
- Pepper
- Strong herbs (rosemary is very nice, as well as thyme and sage)
- Lemon, for putting a bit of lemon juice at the very end
- Oil
- **IF GOING EXTRA FANCY**: parmesan cheese. Any type of dry cheese, like romano or pecorino, will work as well. Even some dry french cheeses, such as grated Comte or Emmental, will work, but be careful, those cheeses are definitely a bit stinkier!

Mix all seasonings in the flour, as well as in the breadcrumb mix if you feel like it. Beat the eggs in a separate bowl, creating eggwash. Dice the chicken and zucchini. Cover them in the flour, then in the eggwash, then finally in the breadcrumbs. Fry them in oil; if you have a lot of oil to spare, deep fried is ideal, but if not then pan fried will also work. No matter what, you will want to use a decent amount of oil in the pan, as you want the optimum crispiness for your Po Boy filling.

Once the color is golden brown, voila! Your filling is ready.

<u>The remoulade:</u>

Remoulades can get very complicated very quickly, which is why I will try to keep mine simple. But even by keeping it simple, it is definitely still using quite a few ingredients! If you are very broke, just simple mayonnaise will work. Still, if you can add something to the mayo, even if it is just lemon juice, salt and pepper, that is definitely better than just plain mayo! If too broke for mayo, make your own on page xx.

You will need:
- Mayo
- Worcestershire sauce
- White wine vinegar (if not lemon juice is fine)
- Hot sauce
- Garlic, minced
- Spices
- Herbs (my favorite is sage, but experimenting with different herbs is fine. Scallions or ciboulette herbs work amazing as well)

- Mustard, (ideally Creole mustard or French old fashioned mustard, but something is better than nothing in this case, again)

Mix all ingredients, until the remoulade sauce has become homogeneous. Voila! The remoulade is made. You want a vibrant pink/red color, so if you do not have that don't hesitate to add more hot sauce. The remoulade is definitely meant to be spicy.

Finally assembling the Po Boy:
Cut the bread in half, toast it if you would like (I recommend to do so). Smear some remoulade on both sides of it, add the filling, and there you go! An amazing, delicious, cheap Po Boy. Serve with the leftover remoulade on the side, I can honestly never get enough of that stuff.
Enjoy the Po Boy! It is definitely one of the higher-end meals I will have in a month, since I like using Chicken for this dish, but there are many ways to make it much cheaper, as stated above. This cheap sandwich is seriously filling, so do try it!

**Tomato carpaccio**

What I love about this dish is its simplicity. But trust me, it is absolutely delicious! Ideally, use olive oil for this dish, but as I know that olive oil is expensive and could ruin your budget I completely understand if using flavored oils makes more sense. Flavored oils are incredibly easy to make, too: you can make your own chili garlic oil by just heating up the oil at a low temperature with garlic and whole chilies for a couple of hours. You can also just let the garlic and chilis sit inside the oil for a couple of days, the oil will eventually become more and more flavored. Makes for a delicious pungent spicy oil; no need to use good oil for this, either. Another great variant is herb oil: just blend up all of those leftover herbs that you have before they turn bad with some oil: you will obtain an incredibly green oil, which looks great on salads. Anyways, here is one of the simplest recipes in the book, which works even better with good quality tomatoes. If not, do not worry, the end result is always delicious no matter what :)

You can add mozzarella to this dish, sliced thinly as well, but as good mozzarella can be expensive and you definitely don't want to be using the cheap kind I will make that ingredient optional. If you want to use some at least decent mozzarella for splurge budget reasons, then no problem, as the cheese can definitely enhance the dish.

Tomato carpaccio:
- Tomatoes
- Olive Oil (or one of the flavored oils I talked about)
- Salt
- Pepper
- Basil (optional)
- Mozzarella (optional)
- Oregano (optional)
- Reduced balsamic vinegar (expensive so optional)

Slice the tomatoes as thinly as you can, and lay them out. Drizzle with olive oil, salt, pepper, shredded basil (optional) and oregano leaves (optional). If using mozzarella,slice thinly as well and assemble: one slice of tomato, then one slice of mozzarella, then one slice of tomato, and so on.

The result will be absolutely delicious. This is one of those recipes that are almost too good to be true. If you are looking for a bit more to this simple dish, because the tomatoes are not too good, toasted sesame seeds sprinkled on top are a great way to add some flavor if needed. Some people use lemon juice, and/or balsamic vinegar, I believe that it ruins the natural acidity of the tomatoes. However, reduced balsamic vinegar can add some sweetness to the dish, which some people definitely appreciate. Just drizzle a tiny bit over the tomato carpaccio, if desired. Not too much! You don't want the dish to be overly sweet either. To make the reduced balsamic, just cook down some balsamic vinegar on low heat until it is thick and syrupy. Done. Delicious tomato carpaccio, great for parties as well! :p

**Risotto/Jambalaya**

Everyone insists that risotto is a fancy dish. They will also tell you that risotto is very expensive to make. And, normally, it is! All famous chefs will tell you that you need this special Italian arborio rice (around 10 dollars a ½ kilo bag!), and then you will need some stock, white wine, a little butter, and most importantly lots and lots of Parmesan cheese. Then, on top of all of this you need to add something fancy in your risotto, like a whole medley of mushrooms, or some asparagus, or some type of seafood which is usually expensive. Honestly, I will admit: for the best risotto you will ever taste, you absolutely need all of these fancy ingredients, I am not denying that. However, you can still make incredibly tasty risotto, even without these ingredients. It won't taste as good as if you had used the fancy chef ingredients, but in my opinion it is honestly still the next best thing. You can also see up there that I mentioned Jambalaya. This will truly depend on what types of ingredients you have at hand. You want to sound fancy when making your dishes, and in my opinion both risotto and Jambalaya sound fancy. I would argue that Jambalaya is even a bit easier to make than risotto, but risotto is slightly better for those "fancy" dinner occasions. However, Risotto will tend to require a more expensive element (cheese) which Jambalaya does not. Also, depending on the kind of rice you have, it may be better suited for Jambalaya, or vice-versa, risotto. Risotto is meant to be goopy (but not like soup, more of a porridge consistency), whereas Jambalaya is more of a baked rice dish. So depending on how sticky your rice is, you may want to opt one way or another. No matter what, any type of cheese will usually make any type of rice sticky enough to pass as risotto. If it does not, there is always the option to add a teeny bit of flour or cornstarch, to make the risotto stick together a bit better. Anyways, here are the two recipes:

Risotto:

You will need:
- Rice
- Some stock (homemade is ideal, but bouillon cubes work as well (recipe for stock pg 70). Choose the type of stock based on preference

and type of risotto you are making. Seafood stock is ideal for seafood risotto, for example)
- White wine
- An onion
- Celery (optional)
- Parsley and/or Sage (Optional)
- Cheese (ideally parmesan, but really any cheese will work I promise)
- Oil
- Salt, pepper
- Butter (just one knob will be enough, if you have more that's better)
- Fillings (3 different ideas after the simple risotto recipe)

Dice the onion. Add oil to the pan (ideally olive oil or a teeny bit of oil and some butter, it really depends what ingredients are at hand here. Just remember to add some butter at the end for the finishing touch!). Cook the onions until almost translucent, on medium high heat. Add rice and a teeny bit of salt. Cook until rice starts to brown, stirring constantly. Add a bit of white wine, and keep stirring. Add the stock, one ladle at a time, stirring constantly. You don't want your risotto to burn! You can alternate between white wine and stock every 3 ladles of stock added, if you have enough wine at hand. Taste the rice as you are stirring, making sure that the rice is neither too cooked nor not cooked enough. You could be stirring for up to 40 minutes, depending on the rice you are using. So be prepared with enough stock for this dish, that's all. If using filling and not just plain risotto, make sure to add the filling at some point during this process.

Once the rice has achieved desired consistency, finish with garnish: remove pan from heat and add chopped herbs, cheese, pepper, and that knob of butter. Stir one last time and cover for about 15-30 seconds, allowing the cheese to melt properly. Serve with grated cheese on top, if possible.

I will give an idea for 3 fillings: one is seafood (mussels, as they are some of the cheapest seafood available in Boston), one is vegetable, one is mushroom (you can find some seriously cheap mushrooms in the Asian market, I promise! My favorite cheap mushrooms are enoki and simple white mushrooms (champignons de Paris, to be exact).

Seafood filling:
Wash then boil the mussels, with just water, celery, carrot, onion, garlic white wine, some hot sauce, salt, and herbs if you have. My favorite for this is sage and bay leaves, but experiment with different herbs until you find something absolutely amazing. You can also add Safran, but seeing how expensive this is maybe it

may be smarter to add something else that is red, such as cayenne pepper or Cajun spice.

Once the mussels open, remove the mussels and choose to keep them either in the shell or outside the shell for your risotto. Mussels that never open can be discarded, as this means that they are probably inedible. Keep the water as well, that will be your stock for the risotto


Vegetable filling:

The famous vegetable is asparagus, and even sometimes artichoke when they are in season, but those vegetables are very expensive in my opinion, even when they are in season. Squash and pumpkin for fall season tends to be very cheap, especially when buying at Haymarket. But honestly, any vegetable that still can achieve some sort of crunch even after it is cooked should be great for this dish. In summer, for example, a nice arugula and kohlrabi risotto is amazing. Just add the arugula at the very end, at the same time as the parmesan. Cook the vegetables with some chopped garlic, until you get that much desired golden brown color that everyone yearns for. Add some rosemary, if possible. Add salt and pepper to finish the filling. Again, make sure to add the filling at the end of the risotto cooking process.

Mushroom filling:
 Cook the mushrooms with some garlic, until golden brown. Add salt and pepper at the end. I like to add some lemon juice at the end too, then toss some breadcrumbs and toast them as well. This is not at all necessary. Add the mushroom filling when the risotto is almost finished being cooked.


This shows three simple examples which can be used to make absolutely mouth-watering risotto. I love risotto because it is the pinnacle of Italian cuisine. All Italians will really put it in your face that all ingredients are needed to make the dish, but honestly I have made great risotto with cheap ingredients. Sorry, Italians, my risotto may not be as good as yours, but considering mine costs less than one dollar to make it's pretty darn good I would say.



Jambalaya

Jambalaya is very similar to risotto, but it is not gloopy like risotto. There is also no cheese, ever, making it cheaper than risotto. It is a Caribbean dish, making it generally an affordable dish, and is usually served with beans. It is similar to risotto in the sense that you toast the rice a bit first before you add the water. But here, you don't need to stir the rice constantly after adding the water/stock. This makes the dish a lot simpler to make, also a lot less work. Unlike risotto, it is generally served with meat or sausage inside it. Putting meat and sausage will make it taste best, but yet again is unnecessary and will taste just fine without. Spices are what will make this dish truly pop. Seafood Jambalaya is also a great idea, if you have the means of affording it. I would recommend mussels again for this one, but the classic seafood jambalaya in my opinion is with shrimp. Depending on the region where you are living, shrimp may be cheaper than mussels! So always be sure to watch out for the good deals :)

Jambalaya:
- Oil
- Onion
- Tomato
- Rice
- Celery (optional)
- Carrots (optional)
- Spices (I recommend paprika, parsley, some cayenne pepper, and cumin. Many combinations are possible, always remember! Jerk spice is equally amazing)
- Chicken stock (optional)
- Sausage (optional)
- Salt and pepper

Dice the onions, celery (optional) and carrots (optional). Cook on medium high heat, until onions are translucent. Add rice, tomato , spices, and sausage (optional), and cook until rice is golden brown.
Add water, this time all of the water at once. It will be for one cup of rice around one cup and a half of water. You can also use chicken stock, or any stock for that matter. Add salt and pepper. Cover the rice pot, and turn down the heat to very low. Let cook for 20-30 minutes, or until rice has absorbed all of the water in the pot.
Boom! You just made Jambalaya! If you like the bottom of your pot to be that extra brown crispy rice, just turn up the heat a little bit towards the end, to medium. It will take a lot of practice to get that bottom crispy without the rice burning. It can also be easier or harder to have the rice burn, depending on the rice you are using. No matter how it turns out, remember, next time you are more experienced and ready to try again! As a rule however, for the crispy rice I would say 15-20 minutes on low heat, depending on the rice that you are using.

**BEANS SECTION**

Now, what goes better with Jambalaya than beans? No joke, beans were part of my staple dinner for at least 2 months. I got so broke at some point that I started adding beans onto everything, even pasta! I made bean dip for chips, beans on rice, beans on pasta, bean chili soup… beans are just amazing. My favorite are the black beans, because they are high in protein content and taste better in my opinion. However, many types of beans can be used: black eyed peas, red kidney beans, those white 'cannellini' beans… but in my experience the best price-to-flavor ratio beans must be the black beans. I love garbanzo beans as well, and they are overall cheap, but I would usually make other different recipes with Garbanzo beans (also called chickpeas). With chickpeas, I would make a lot of different stews and salads, but they are a mediterranean bean, whereas the beans for the recipes below tend to be caribbean/central american/south american beans. Feel free to use chickpeas however, if those are the only beans that you have on hand for the moment.

The big secret for making beans cheap: don't buy them canned! Canned beans are incredibly cheap, sure, but dried beans are so much cheaper. With canned beans, you are paying extra for having them boil the beans, adding salt to them, and then sticking them in an aluminium container (the can)! Dried beans usually come in large quantities: a 5 dollar bag should easily last you a good month or so. And that 5 dollar bag has the equivalent of at least 20 cans! So dried beans are definitely cheaper.

Dried beans however take a lot more time to prepare: you have to rehydrate them then boil them, sometimes for many hours depending on the bean you choose.
However, this book is about saving every penny possible, and indeed buying dried beans in the long run will help you save a lot of money, and make it more likely for you to stick to your 20 dollar a week food budget.

Rehydrate the dried beans overnight, with a bit of salt and a pinch of baking soda (if you have some, this is again optional. I always relied on my neighbors for that pinch of baking soda, they probably knew what I was coming for every time I knocked on that door. We are still cool with each other, so no hard feelings old neighbor!). Then, boil the beans until they are soft enough to your liking. Some people like them as soft as if it were coming from a can, some people a bit more firm than that, some a bit more soft than that. It also depends on the recipe. I will be using firm, medium, or soft beans, depending on the recipe.
No matter what, keep those beans in that bean water! You can prepare a lot of beans in advance, and just keep them in the pot and refrigerate that. It should be good for 3 days or so. Also, there is flavor + nutrients in that bean water! You can legit use this for thickening soups, making sauces, deglazing pans, and

a bunch of other things! So keep the bean water, it is useful! Anyways, time for some recipes:

**SIMPLE BEAN SIDE** (delicious on rice, or even by its own really)
Mexicans would call this refried beans, but I think of it as a simple bean side. It is just too simple and too delicious for what it is. It's almost a trick for how good this bean side is. The recipe:
Bean side:
- Beans, medium (preferably black beans)
- Garlic
- Oil
- Lime juice
- Cilantro (coriander leaf)
- Salt
- Cumin (optional)
- Optional but fancy last minute garnishes: Queso Fresco, as well as a teeny bit of butter. You can also finish with some crispy bacon bits, some people like that but I try to keep it kosher :)

Chop garlic. Heat pan on high heat, add oil. Put chopped garlic into hot oil, until you can really smell it, but don't let it brown too much. Add the beans, with a bit of bean water, salt and a pinch or two of cumin (optional). Cook down on medium heat until

desired consistency. Chop Cilantro very roughly (dried cilantro is fine too, I once had coriander seeds and ground them up, it was pretty good on the beans), add once the beans are cooked down to desired consistency. Add lemon juice. Turn off heat. Serve. Finish with one of the optional but fancy (and expensive) last minute garnishes, if you like. I recommend queso fresco but any cheese will be good on top of this. Sour cream is a great option too!
If you have no garnish, do not worry, this dish still ranks as one of my most memorable sides in college. I guess I just really love beans!
This dish is a great side to anything, but I would not recommend having it alone. The beans need to go along with something. Even if it's just toasted bread it will be better than nothing, that's for sure.


## BEAN CHILI

Simple, yet delicious. This is definitely best made with some meat, but as meat is expensive it is absolutely not necessary. All you really need to make chili are some onions and some spices (enough hot sauce will do the trick, but having fresh hot peppers, like jalapenos or habaneros, is ideal. Just remember to dose accordingly depending on how hot your peppers are!) with some beans, but it is definitely possible to have more ingredients into the mix.

Best part about chili is that it is very easy to make. You just stick ingredients in a pot, and boil them down until they become chili. And good chili is delicious. As usual, the cheapest chili you can make requires only 3-4 ingredients, but the tastiest chili will use a couple more ingredients. Fancy garnishes (queso fresco) are possible, but again not necessary. No matter what, Chili in my opinion is a great way to finish the week, as you can add almost all of your leftover herbs and vegetables+meat in the pot, and it will probably taste good. Sometimes there are some random vegetables that you forgot to finish during the past week, plus a little bit of chicken or something. Chili will be able to harmonize all of these ingredients into one big bowl of awesomeness

Chili:
- Beans, soft
- Hot peppers (Chipotle are my favorite because of their smokiness, but Jalapenos, or any chili pepper really, will taste just fine and amazing)
- Onions
- Cumin
- Salt, pepper
- Bell peppers

Optional ingredients:
- Tomatoes
- Corn
- Garlic
- A bit of BBQ sauce

- Beef (or chicken, or any meat actually. All should do the trick. It can be ground or not ground, it seriously does not matter for this one)
- Beef, chicken or vegetable broth
- Red, green, and/or yellow bell peppers
- Coriander (leaves or powder, both work)
- Other vegetables (almost any vegetable will work, seriously)
- Vegetarian meat (tofu, boca crumbles, or other)
- A little bit of amber beer, brown ale, or red wine
- Oregano (leaves or powder, both work)
- Limes (a teeny bit of zest, but the juice is what really matters. If limes are untreated, you can chop them extremely thin and add that to the chili!)
- Bread (as thickener)

Optional garnishes:
- Sour cream
- Cheese
- Coriander leaves
- Diced avocado
- Chopped scallions (or chives even)
- Hot sauce
- Lime juice (or chopped limes)

Chop all of the ingredients to a somewhat even size. Start by cooking the onions with the hot peppers on medium heat, until they are almost translucent. Then, add the meat (optional). Then, add the vegetables, corn, and bell peppers until everything is browned a bit. If you are using tomatoes add them right after the rest of the vegetables are browned. Then, add the beans, cumin and lime and stir for another minute. After, add water (or chicken stock, or beer, or whatever flavorful liquid you want to put in. The bean water is a great idea!) and let cook for 5-10 minutes, until the chili gets thick. You can thicken the chili more if you would like, with bread. Finish with garnish (or garnishes), as well as salt and pepper to taste. Serve.

I have never made 2 chilis taste exactly the same, but all have been delicious. So be creative! Chili will help you clean out all the little pieces left in the fridge, so putting 3 different kinds of meat and garnishing with cream cheese is seriously not terrible at all, and it actually tastes quite good in my opinion. I would have prefered adding sour cream or queso fresco, but sometimes you just can't be too picky, we are living on a 20 dollar budget a week after all.

### Bean fritters

A fritter of anything is pretty good: Oil+salt makes our brains go crazy, which is why we are so addicted to chips, pizza, and other greasy and salty foods. A bean fritter has oil and has salt, so of course it is delicious. For these fritters, surprisingly enough my favorite beans are the black eyed pea beans, but anything is possible of course.

These are incredibly cheap party snacks which definitely need a sauce to be dipped in. a remoulade here works amazing, giving just that little amount of heat and flavor that the dish needs. but many sauces are possible, honestly simple homemade hot sauce should be absolutely incredible for these fritters. Recipe to follow the bean fritter.

Bean fritters:
- Beans, firm
- Flour
- Onion powder (fresh works too)
- Garlic powder (fresh works too)
- Herbs, ideally some nice Rosemary and parsley, but as usual any herb should do the trick
- Spices, ideally turmeric and a bit of Curry, but again most red looking spices will enhance flavor and do the trick. Just limit yourself to a couple of spices! unless you have some experience and knowledge and can already make Indian dishes which require sometimes 12 different spices…
- Egg

- Bean water
- Salt and pepper
- Breadcrumbs(optional)
- Cheese(optional)

Chop everything up finely, and mix in a bowl. add enough flour until you can make solid balls that are not too doughy.

Make the balls, and cover with breadcrumbs if desired (the usual eggwash method, explained in the "rice balls" recipe pg 22).

Fry in hot oil until golden brown.

Serve, with the homemade hot sauce or any other sauces if you would like.

Homemade hot sauce:
- Hot peppers
- Bit of onion
- Bit of garlic
- Parsley and/or coriander, fresh and in seeds for the coriander if possible
- Vinegar
- Teeny bit of mustard seeds (if you have, if not normal mustard should do)
- Salt and pepper

That's it!

Blend everything in a food processor. If you don't have one just chop everything as finely as you can then add lots of the vinegar at the end, in order to make a chunky salsa-type hot sauce. Add some water to the sauce if it is too vinegar-ey. Feel free to char the hot peppers a bit before blending, if you desire more of a smoky flavor.

Enjoy the sauce with the bean fritters, or anything else!

**Bean salad**

What is great about bean salad: you don't need that many ingredients to make it taste good. Great way to accompany any dish. Dressed with an easy vinaigrette, this salad truly embodies fresh, simple, delicious food! To have a little variation of color it is nice to use different kinds of beans for this dish. This is a good dish to make when you have a little bit of different kinds of beans left, in general.

Bean salad:
- Corn (grilled, boiled or canned, it doesn't matter. I personally prefer grilled corn however)
- Beans, medium (more than one type of bean is ideal)
- Tomatoes
- Couscous, cooked (optional; bulgur wheat would also work. Not too much is needed, you want the beans to be the star of the dish!)

- Red onions
- Bell peppers
- Chopped cilantro or parsley
- Lettuce, or salad (optional)
- Salt, pepper
- Lime (optional)

Cube up the tomatoes, bell peppers and red onions. Add beans, corn, couscous (optional) and salad (optional). Finish with chopped herb, salt, pepper, and lime (optional). Dress the salad with some salad dressing, if desired.

Salad dressing:
- Chili oil and/or herb oil 2/3rds
- Vinegar 1/3rd
- Some mustard
- Salt, pepper

Whisk the ingredients, until you have an amazing dressing. With the chili and/or herb oil, it is sure to spice up any salad!

**Bean burger**

Ah, the staple of any vegetarian! All meat lovers think of these burger patties as absolute junk, but something undeniable is that bean burgers are way cheaper than actual meat burgers. I know it seems like that is not the case when you buy bean burgers pre-made and frozen, but trust me, make them yourself and you will see just how cheap they actually are.

- Beans, firm
- Flour (ideally breadcrumbs instead of flour)
- Garlic
- Onion
- Corn
- Spices (namely cumin, but curry and turmeric are a great replacement. If you like spicy add some spice!)
- Egg
- Herbs (I usually put some parsley, but as usual any herb is better than no herb)
- Salt, pepper

Make sure to drain as much water from the beans as possible, nobody likes mushy bean burgers. Chop the garlic and onion very finely, as well as the herbs. Mix them with the beans, breadcrumbs (or flour), spices, salt, and corn. Form nice patties with the mixture obtained.

Fry the patties nicely on both sides, until golden brown. Don't cook for too long, or else the patties get too firm.

If you make the patties thin enough, they can actually fit in the toaster! Then it's about 3-4 minutes in the toaster, and you are all set :)

You can serve the burger with a toasted bun and some condiments (pickles, tomato, lettuce, etc.), but this is cheap cooking, usually I will have the bean burger patty on its own or with some sauce (ketchup, bbq sauce, or curry remoulade (mayo, curry, salt, chili flakes)). The burger is absolutely incredible with a simple cabbage slaw, which is incredibly cheap.

**For the slaw:** mayo, cabbage, salt, lemon juice, minced garlic (optional), spices (optional) Chop the cabbage finely. and add all of the other ingredients in a different bowl and mix, then put into the cabbage. You have yourself a nice slaw now!

To make this a full meal: rice, pasta or bread will do the trick. Bread is ideal, but sometimes we are broke and need to resort to other options. Totally understandable, as that is the nature of this book! If it needs to be rice or pasta, just be sure to season it a bit, so that it does not taste bland. No matter what, that bean burger is delicious and packed with flavor and nutrients, so it's a great way to stay full for the day (or the night, if you are going out)!

**Tempura**

What I love about Tempura batter is that it is so simple and cheap to make, yet everyone thinks of it as fancy and expensive. I guess it all depends on what you fry. Making shrimp tempura is definitely more expensive than broccoli tempura, which is almost just as delicious.

My first week of having my first kitchen in college (so 2nd year of college, the 1st year of college I was on the meal plan), I wowed everyone I was living with using this recipe. It was incredibly cheap, and one of the roommates had loads of baking soda and soda water so I did not need to even buy that. I got a couple of zucchinis for one dollar, and blew them away by how good the tempura was. They had no way to even describe it, besides the fact that it was delicious! Served with rice, this dish can be a full meal for sure.

Basically, tempura will work on any not too flaky fish, but most vegetables can be fried and be absolutely delicious. Again, anything battered and fried tends to be delicious.

The biggest secret to having amazing tempura is actually making sure the batter is ice cold, it needs to be ice water. We are looking for the airiest batter in the world, and having extremely cold batter collide with the extremely hot oil makes the air expand more, and the batter airier. I will be using soda water (or seltzer water) to make an even airier batter, but using normal water should still make this dish taste like tempura, as long as the water used is ice cold

Tempura:
- Soda Water, or seltzer water (any sparkling water, really).
- Ice

- Flour
- Salt
- Baking soda
- Oil
- Whatever you want to fry. I highly recommend vegetables and certain seafood, like shrimp, and would avoid frying meat if it is of a high enough quality. However, tofu tempura is delicious in my opinion!

Mix flour, salt, baking soda, water, and ice. Make sure the batter is not too thick but not too thin. Use a cold bowl to start with, if possible. Also, there should still be chunks of ice inside the batter while you are frying.

Heat up pot of oil. Dip whatever you want to fry in the cold batter, then straight into the hot oil.

Fry until golden brown, or even slightly before that to make it look the same color as in the japanese restaurants. Serve with tempura sauce

TEMPURA SAUCE: just mix all ingredients. You can play with the proportions, and some ingredients are optional:
- Soy Sauce
- Rice wine vinegar (lemon juice can do the trick as well)
- Honey (sugar works just as well. Ideally not brown sugar however)
- Ginger (optional)

- Tiny bit of Pineapple juice (optional)
- Garlic (optional)
- Teeny bit of worcestershire sauce (optional)

Boom! Delicious tempura! It is an absolutely delicious snack, starter to a meal, or hors d'oeuvre in my opinion.

Tempura is again one of those dishes that you make when you have a lot of variety in your fridge. If there are many different vegetables, then it makes a lot of sense to make this dish. Especially because all of the other ingredients required for the dish are usually readily available in the kitchen.

## Fish tacos

Now, I know that fish can be expensive. But you know what is incredibly cheap? Tortillas. If you get the mexican corn tortillas in bulk, the big advantage they will have over bread is that they will stay fresh for a very long time as long as they are not removed from the bag. If they are stale, fry them! Homemade tortilla chips are always delicious, with a little bit of salt :)

Sometimes, there will be fish specials in the supermarket. This is usually because the fish is getting old, and the market wants to sell that fish quickly. It may not be fresh off the boat fish, but the fish is definitely more than edible, and most importantly, it will be cheap. 4 dollars of fish are probably enough for 2-3 good meals for one person. Great for dinner parties, as everyone thinks you are being fancy doing this. This cheap fish may be a little fishy, which is why the perfect way to mask this fishiness is to fry the fish and make fish tacos, adding a lot of flavor along the way.

What I love about fish tacos are their versatility and their simplicity. It's just fried fish with some cabbage and some sauce (sometimes 2 sauces), but oh man is it delicious. Anyways, here is the recipe:

For the fish:
- Corn tortilla
- Fish, sliced into chunks. Remove the bones if you can; if not, some people in Thailand actually eat the bones for calcium intake, so it's up to you if you like bone or not. Be sure to chew well if you decide to eat the fish bone. I will always remember working in that thai restaurant where everyone would eat the fish whole with the bone, and always look at me strange for taking the time to fillet the fish. I was the strange person in the Thai restaurant because I was eating the fish without any bones!
- Flour
- Salt, spices for the flour(I would usually go with cumin, pepper, teeny bit of cayenne, and coriander seeds if I am lucky. But seriously make what you want! lemon/lime zest work

great, and once I used steak seasoning in the flour and it was actually pretty good. Just remember to add some seasonings to your flour)

For the slaw:
- Cabbage (green is ideal, some people do a mix with red cabbage but no need to)
- Grated carrot (optional, and need very little carrots anyways)
- Minced red onion (optional, and really don't need a lot)
- Coriander leaves/cilantro (optional, and really don't need a lot)
- Queso fresco (optional). Any cheeze will work, but this is a fish taco so queso fresco is ideal. Remember to try new things!

For the IMPORTANT sauce (garlic aioli):
- Mayonnaise
- Garlic
- Lime juice (lemon juice can work as well)
- Salt
- Pepper (optional)

Mince the garlic. Add it to the mayo, and then add the other ingredients. Make sure it is neither too thick nor too runny, but don't worry it SHOULD definitely be a pretty runny sauce

For the OPTIONAL sauces:

Chipotle sauce:

- Chipotle tabasco (if you have real chipotle peppers, it is better but those are usually hard to find. (also expensive). If you do have that just use a bit of the chipotle pepper and douse it in white wine vinegar. Lemon/lime juice can also do the trick))
- Diced Tomato
- Diced onion
- Cilantro, chopped
- Garlic, minced
- Salt

Just mix and season to taste. Lime juice at the end can be a good idea

Pico de gallo:
- Tomato, garlic, onion, jalapeno, salt, cilantro (optional). Dice everything up small and wow is this delicious every time

Salsa verde:
- Tomatillos, roasted jalapenos (just stick that straight on the burner to char it), salt, pepper, lime juice, onion (optional). Blend that in a mixer and you are all set! Season to taste

Douse the fish in the seasoned flour, covering it all. Fry the chunks of fish, getting color until the fish is soft and moist. Then, heat the tortillas in the same pan (or a different one, or even straight on the burner if you like, but the tacos get more flavor if heated up from same pan). Then have the cabbage, sauce (or sauces), and all other condiments on the side. Make sure to have plenty of lime wedges as well, to spray over the fish. I usually put the cabbage in the taco first, then the fish, then spray some lime juice on the fish, then the sauce(s) then top with the condiments (cilantro and/or minced onion 90% of the time in Mexico)

This taco seriously tastes like heaven. It is one of the most exciting dishes I can make during the month, just because it is so freaking good. In general, I guess that I am ecstatic whenever I can afford fish, it just adds a new dimension to my life. But whenever I do get fish, this dish is the one that makes me most excited because it is so homey: lots of small plates, that we just pass around one another in order to serve everybody. I hope you are fans of this dish as much as I am!

## BREADED CHICKEN/EGGPLANT

This recipe will teach you the classic way to bread absolutely anything. I am using chicken and/or eggplant as an example, as later I will show the extension of this which will be chicken/eggplant parm (which itself can be transformed into a sub sandwich) but seriously, you can bread almost anything using this technique. Once I breaded Zucchini, once I breaded a turnip. Surprisingly enough, it was all delicious. Don't go too crazy, but even if you do it might still taste good! Some people like breaded ice cream or breaded chocolate, no joke. Just make sure the batter is thick enough when you do this, and don't add too much extra flavor in the breadcrumbs, keep it simpler for these (although chili in breaded chocolate is a classic and a great idea. Mint too). I was actually thinking about breading some bread sometime, I bet that would actually taste quite good, thanks to the difference in textures and all that. Anyways, here is the recipe and some sauce ideas:

Breading:
- Breadcrumbs (soft or hard, depending on what you are making and what the goal is)
- Eggwash (just an egg or two, beaten)
- Flour
- Salt, pepper
- Spices (depending on what you are breading, try different spices. Depending on which sauce as well. No matter what, you can't go wrong with some smoked paprika that's for sure
- Herbs (same as spices, but parsley is good on almost every type of food)
- Grated cheese (optional, ideally parmesan with a big emphasis on using that one)
- Whatever you are breading

Put whatever you are breading into the flour, which is just seasoned with salt and pepper, then into the eggwash, then into the breadcrumbs which are mixed with all of the herbs and all of the spices, as well as the grated cheese (optional). Repeat several times, if you want a thicker crust, but 95% of the time I believe there will be enough breading with only one coating.

Fry in frying pan, until whatever in the middle is cooked. If the thing is too big and the breadcrumbs are already golden brown, finish the cooking in the oven. To make the breading extra crispy, you can toast the breadcrumbs before breading the ingredients. It makes a really nice texture.

Voila! You have a breaded masterpiece of something (or many different things for that matter). My two favorite things to bread are chicken and eggplant. Zucchini is also pretty darn delicious. Don't bread expensive stuff like beef or really good fish, because they are so good on their own they don't need all of this stuff to stand out. You can put some type of crust on these expensive ingredients, like a pistachio and walnut crust, but if you desperately need the crust then sprinkle it on top and finish those nice dishes in the oven. It makes for a more elegant dish.

If you don't have egg and flower, just use the breadcrumbs as seasoning; the breadcrumbs impart flavor, and depending on what we are breading we must add more or less flavor to these breadcrumbs.

Try many different combinations until you find and know what you like. My favorite is always keeping it simple: breadcrumbs, salt pepper, parsley, garlic and onion powder, and if we have it, parmesan cheese. All of this mixed into the breadcrumbs tastes like heaven to me, that is one thing for sure!

Finally, try different types of breadcrumbs: soft breadcrumbs, hard breadcrumbs, fresh breadcrumbs, panko breadcrumbs, breadcrumbs made with baguette, semmel breadcrumbs (famous being used for the Austrian dish Weiner Schnitzel), and the list goes on and on. But what matters most, is that you have breadcrumbs!


MAKE IT CHICKEN/EGGPLANT PARM:
Just before the chicken, eggplant or whatever else you are breading is fully cooked, add some mozzarella cheese on top, then stick it in the oven until the cheese has melted. Once the cheese is nicely melted, stick the fried cheesy goodness on a plate and douse it with marinara sauce. Boom! 5-star restaurant level eggplant or chicken parm has just been served!

**Awesome jacket potatoes**
For this recipe, you ideally want large potatoes, but honestly any potato will do the trick. I like potatoes because they are cheap and actually very healthy, as long as you don't put too much oil on them (like fries

and chips, literally covered in oil). I believe that a jacket potato is a great dish which can be infinitely versatile: it is just a baked potato with whatever you decide to put in it! I am giving one simple example of one of the cheapest jacket potatoes you can make, but remember that you can always be creative. Especially with this recipe, almost any ingredient can be swapped for some other one. Just remember to have that balance of salt, veggies and fat!

One large potato: bake it in the oven on high heat, for about 30-45 minutes (depends on the size of the potato). Essentially you want to bake the potato until the crust is nice and tough, and the middle is extremely fluffy.

Then, slit the top of the potato and open it up. Fill the potato with whatever filling you would like, and boom! The perfect jacket potato pops into existence I have put some ideas for great fillings, which are incredibly cheap, but always feel free to make your own creations!

<u>Filling 1:</u>
- Broccoli, chopped finely
- Green beans, blanched for a bit (10-20 seconds) and cut into small pieces
- Onions, chopped
- Garlic, chopped
- Salt, pepper
- Scallions
- Some sour cream (optional)

- Acid, so lemon juice or vinegar drops it doesn't matter really

Cook the broccoli, green beans, onions and garlic until onions become translucent. Add a bit of salt. Cool mixture, then mix with sour cream, lime juice, scallions, salt and pepper. You can also add some shredded carrots and bacon if you want to. Pour mixture on top of opened jacket potato.

Filling 2: just cheese and herbs
Cheese is delicious! Why complicate something that doesn't need to be complicated? We are eating on a budget after all.

Filling 3: meat
I believe that ground beef is ideal, and if it is leftover you can actually open the potato slightly in advance and stick this bad boy in for some color. Remember to add seasoning! Cheese and sour cream compliments this well, but most important in my opinion would be to have some cooked translucent onion in there

Filling 4:
Mix filling 1, 2 and/or 3! Trust me, it is absolutely to die for :)

Filling 5: butter

Potato and butter, with salt pepper and herbs? I promise, simplicity can go a long way if the potato is cooked perfectly. You can always replace the butter with olive oil, but when living on the line trust me butter tastes better and can be cheaper.

My point is, with a well cooked potato you can stick almost anything inside of it, and it will taste absolutely fabulous. Experiment with whatever you have in the house for some tasty combinations! Although a chocolate and marshmallow jacket potato does not sound too appealing to me, who knows, maybe the starchiness mixed with the sweet and a bit of salt and butter tastes really good… only one way to find out!

**Crepes**
Everyone thinks of crepes as fancy, but did you know it is really only 3 ingredients? Milk, flour, egg. That's it. Some people add more things to their crepes, some don't. But those three ingredients are all you need, maybe with a pinch of salt. I add water to my crepes, because I like my crepes extra thin and can make more crepes out of one batch this way.

Don't worry, the first couple of crepes will most likely get messed up, but in the long run you will get good at flipping the crepes.

I always eyeball how much of each ingredient is needed, but no matter what: too thick, add water, too thin add a teeny bit of flour. That's all you really need to know.

To make it a full meal, you can fill up your crepe! Classic is ham and cheese with a bit of butter, but you can definitely get creative. If making the crepe savory, it may be best to add a bit more salt in the crepe dough, and even try different flours like whole grain flour or something, adding more flavor to the crepe itself. Of course, cheaper is our goal, so really all you need to do is ensure that everything stays cheap

<u>Crepes:</u>
- Flour
- Milk (any milk will work, even almond milk or soy milk)
- Egg
- Some oil, for the pan

Mix flour and milk first, ensuring no granules or lumps are leftover. Then crack some eggs into the mixture. Add that pinch of salt. If too thick, add some water. I always add water because we are cooking for cheap.

Heat up the pan, really make it scorching hot. Add oil to the pan and spread it around. I learned that cutting the side of a pear and sticking it on a fork to spread the oil on the pan works quite well. The side of an onion works well, too, if you are making savory crepes.

Drop the batter into the pan, making sure that the whole pan is covered. Then once there is no runny liquid in the pan, time to flip it. Run the spatula around the pan, unsticking the crepe from the pan. With practice, you will be able to flip the crepe in the air and make it land on the other side that needs to be cooked.

At this point, if you want to add the filling, this is the time to add the filling (unless it is something cold like whipped cream or ice cream or something). Close the crepe if there is filling, and serve. I love confectioner's sugar on my crepes, but that is always too expensive so i just use normal sugar and am still a very happy man.

Make sure to oil the pan properly after every crepe! Or else it will stick to the pan!

Savory filling ideas:
- Cheese, ham, salted butter
- Cheese, herbs (like parsley), salted butter
- Cheese ground beef, salted butter
- Cheese, egg, salted butter, herbs (like parsley). You can add tomato on this one, some people like that. harissa is great too
- Cheese, mushrooms, salted butter, herbs, harissa (can add more things if you would like)

- Tomato, sausage, thyme, salted butter, parsley, garlic (cook it all together before adding as filling to the crepe)

Sweet ideas for crepes:
- Sugar and lemon (could add nuts and herbs for extra kick)
- Nutella and bananas (chocolate chips are nice too)
- Caramelized apples (recipe pg. 94)
- Oranges, flambeed with grand marnier and sugar (classical French preparation, replace the Grand marnier with almost any booze, even white wine and it will still taste good
- Cheese nuts and honey. It is best to use goat cheese in this case, for sure

Try as many combinations as you like for this, but when it comes to classics there is not too much variation that can be made in my opinion. The French are puritan when it comes to food, after all. I definitely experienced this growing up in France. However, in my opinion: as long as the end result is delicious and satisfying to you, put whatever you want inside your crepe!

**Pumpkin soup**

One of my favorite parts of the fall/ halloween season is just the rise of new fall vegetables. I definitely only eat pumpkin during this period of time, mainly because it is so cheap around fall season. Farmers, especially at the end of the fall season, just want to get rid of the excess pumpkins. There are many college campuses which just give out free pumpkins, too.

My point is, finding pumpkins around October should be easy and cheap. SO, you should be eating a lot of pumpkin during the fall season, for sure. Many ways to prepare it, but the most classical (and one of my favorite) ways is pumpkin soup. So creamy and velvety, I love it. It almost reminds me of carrot soup, to be honest. I like to flavor mine with ginger, for a kick, but a lot of people like cinnamon for some reason. I feel like then the soup tastes just like cinnamon and not like pumpkin when people do this. But, of course, like any of my recipes, you are more than welcome to try!

Pumpkin soup:
- Pumpkin flesh. Keep the seeds and the outside of the pumpkin, you can use the pumpkin shell as a bowl or carve it and make a jack o lantern!
- Pumpkin seeds
- Onions
- Ginger

- Garlic
- Salt
- Vinegar (the more neutral the better)
- Veggie stock (or just water)
- White wine (optional)
- Herbs (thyme, parsley are ideal)
- Butter (if not, substitute for oil)
- Cream (ideally creme fraiche, but any cream will work. Yogurt also does the trick. Optional)
- Croutons (they taste best when you make them yourself! Just put some oil in a frying pan, fry until golden brown and sprinkle with salt (or garlic salt) at the end)

Chop up the pumpkin into cubes. Dice the onion. Fry onion on medium heat until translucent, then add the pumpkin, garlic and ginger. Add some salt. When the pumpkin browns, add some vinegar and white wine (optional) to deglaze the pan. Then you can add some water (or veggie stock if you prefer more flavor), until the desired amount of soup that you want. Simmer for about 10-20 mins, until all pumpkin pieces are soft and can be broken down easily with a spoon. Add the herbs during the simmering process. Then, add the soup mixture into the blender. Blend until a smooth, creamy texture. It is ok to over-blend in this case, shouldn't change the consistency too much. Add some butter at the end of the blending process, or oil, to thicken it up a bit more. No need for too much, but you definitely want some fat in that soup.

Finish with the herbs, croutons, and cream (optional) and serve.

This soup is the best appetizer you will ever have! Goes great with a squash pasta dinner: just squash, garlic and cheese over some perfectly cooked pasta. Some people add cherry tomatoes, but we are too poor for that. It is still absolutely delicious!

**Rosti**

There really are 1000 ways to make potatoes, and if you buy one of those giant bags of potatoes in order to save money, then indeed a lot of potatoes need to be used. I like this recipe a lot because of how simple it is, yet how delicious it is as well. You don't even need to serve much on the side with this delicious potato cake: just some "creme fraiche" with chives or green onions, or some yogurt with dill, will be absolutely incredible. Ketchup definitely also works for this dish as well!

Some people mix with a little bit of flour, I do not. I still believe that the starch of the potato itself is enough to make everything stick into one harmonious piece.

Rosti:
- Potato
- Oil for pan frying
- Salt

Shred the potato pretty thick, using the large teeth on your cheese grater. Wash in cold water and shake, removing as much starch from the potato as possible. No need to remove too much, as then the potato shreddings won't stick to each other anymore, but definitely wash 2-3 times.
Make some thin patties with the potato shreddings, almost like pancakes. Add some salt. Cook 5-10 minutes on each side at medium-high heat, until golden brown. Add some salt at the end. Serve with sauce. The classical sauce is just creme fraiche and chives, but there are many other cheap delicious creamy sauces that you can put on your rosti. Ideally, you want it to be no thinner than ketchup, so it can really cover the whole potato when you dip it in. My ideas:
- Mustard mayonnaise (mix the two)
- Thick dijon mustard, (or old fashioned mustard, with all of the mustard seeds)
- Ketchup
- Spiced ketchup (add chili or hot sauce to the ketchup)
- Yogurt with herbs, and maybe a touch of lemon juice (dill and/or parsley is really nice)

- Tomato sauce
- Remoulade
- Any sauce your heart desires!

**Rosh Hashanah special**
This may be expensive, but for celebration I am ok with this: the tradition is to dip some apples in honey, but what if we added just a bit more? Here is a nice flavored version I have come up with:
RH special:
- Yogurt
- Honey
- Pinch of salt
- Apples
- Thyme, rosemary or mint (up to you, but choose just one only is best)
- Nuts (optional, everything but peanuts I would say. Best are pine nuts or walnuts. Even better if you toast the nuts!)

Cube up the apples, then dip them in honey for the mitzvah. Add the yogurt, herb and a pinch of salt. Mix around until homogeneous. Add nuts (optional, not peanuts though trust me) Voila! Delicious yogurt is served, and a mitzvah is fulfilled at the same time! Everybody wins it seems :)

## Rice Soup

This rice soup may sound pretty nasty, but is definitely one of the best things you can do with leftover rice, or just any rice in general. This is a huge staple dish all across Asia, from China to Thailand. It is great mainly because it can be used as the "end of the week" soup, where all meat scraps and small abandoned bits of vegetables can marry together and make a spectacular dish. What truly makes this dish special will be the broth and the toppings you decide to put on top of it. My personal favorite toppings are fried garlic and onion, with green onions, cilantro, some spice, and a few drops of soy sauce. Also, the choice of broth is pretty important. I like bonito flakes broth personally, as it gives a nice salty flavor to the broth. Some people like miso broth, some people like green tea broth, some people like just simple chicken stock. My favorite is bonito, but using green tea as my broth base is definitely a close second.
The best part about this dish, honestly, is just how filling it is. Rice + hot water= ultimate satisfaction, and definitely a lot cheaper than a bowl of Ramen. Anyways, here is the recipe:

rice soup:
- Rice
- Broth

- Toppings (optional, but my favorite are: chiles, fried shallots and garlic, green onions, cilantro, parsley, and lime juice)
- Food scraps (optional)
- Seaweed (optional)
- Tofu (optional)

Wash the rice, at least three times to get some of that starch out of there and not have the water become too thick and white from the rice starch. cook the rice in the broth, until the rice is perfectly cooked. Add food scraps at this moment, if you have any that are edible. I love to use some leftover leeks or turnips, chop them into thin discs and cook that in the broth for a bit until the vegetables are soft and delicious.
Serve, adding the toppings at the last minute.
There you go, that is all there is to rice soup! I think it is so prevalent in Asia due to Asian cuisine relying on rice a lot, but also because it is such a smart way to recycle leftover rice. So whenever there is a one day old amount of rice in your rice cooker, be sure to reuse it, as rice soup or fried rice or something else! Most important is just making sure that none of the food goes to waste, as wasting food costs money and will eat up your budget, a couple of cents at a time.

**Ratatouille**

I love ratatouille! It screams France and my childhood. Moreover, it is incredibly cheap to make! This is a true "provencal" dish, needing only few ingredients and tastes great on top of rice or alongside pasta, rice or bread. There is no way I will ever get sick of ratatouille, it is too good and cheap!

Ratatouille:
- Zucchini (green, yellow, or both)
- Tomato
- Eggplant
- Bell pepper
- Onion
- Garlic
- Bay leaf (optional)
- Thyme (optional)
- Basil (optional)
- Herbes de provence (ideal, but optional)
- Touch of vinegar (ideally balsamic, but any vinegar will work)
- Salt
- Pepper

Cook the onions on medium heat, until they are translucent. Add the cubed zucchini, eggplant and bell pepper. Cook until brown. Then, add the cubed tomato with the bay leaf. Cook down until the water comes out. Then, add thyme, herbes de provence, salt and pepper to taste. Cook down, until the ratatouille

becomes an amazing stew. Add touch of vinegar. Remove bay leaf at this point.
Serve with chopped basil on top (optional). Best served alongside rice, bread or some nice "provencale" chicken


## "Provencale" chicken:
Great paired with ratatouille. Always brings me back to the south of France
- Chicken
- Tomatoes, roasted in the oven
- Garlic
- Red wine
- Olives
- Anchovies (optional)
- Herbes de provence (optional, just thyme and/or rosemary if you don't have herbes de provence)

Mince the garlic and brown it. Put the chicken in, adding anchovy as well. Once the chicken gets color deglaze the pan with red wine and olives, as well as salt, pepper, herbes de provence and tomato.
Cook down to obtain a rich sauce, and serve alongside ratatouille.
Enjoy an amazing, cheap dinner! The only part that is not cheap here are the olives and anchovies, which can be easily removed from the dish if necessary.

**Chicken or Mutton with peanut butter sauce, on top of rice (jollof or non-jollof)**

My very good friend from Berlin , Robert from Gambia, taught me this recipe. I like it because it is very simple and cheap to get all of the ingredients, yet it is absolutely delicious. You can choose to adjust the amount of spice at will, I recommend one hot pepper per stew which is already plenty, but some people like more spice, which is fine as well. Gambia is a very poor country, with access to meat being rare for most families. This is why it is an incredibly cheap meal, which is also incredibly filling, and does not require meat, only recommends it. You can easily replace the meat with vegetables, like squash, pumpkin, zucchini or something else, if necessary.

The magic of this recipe is the richness of the stew, imparting flavor throughout the whole rice, which can either be white rice or Jollof rice. I recommend to make jollof rice if there are unused leftover ingredients, as a majority of the the ingredients for both dishes are the same, only really needing bell peppers and tomatoes as well. Anyways here is the recipe:

Chicken with peanut butter sauce (called "domoda"):
- 1 onion
- Salt, pepper (preferably white pepper)

- Maggi bouillon cubes (2 or 3)
- One hot pepper, or more depending on how spicy you want it
- Tomato paste
- Tomatoes (optional)
- Garlic (optional)
- Herbs (ideally thyme, but oregano works well, and rosemary works pretty well too. It needs to be a strong herb)
- Peanut butter
- Water
- Chicken, or mutton. The recipe tastes better with mutton but I understand that mutton can be very expensive in some areas of the world, so chicken is just fine. Even if you only have a chicken carcass (or mutton carcass) with very little meat, that is okay it will still make the dish taste better, as the base of this dish is the stew itself. You can even make this optional, replacing the meat with some vegetables. I found that squash works extremely well, but there are many other vegetables that can be used. Just make sure that the vegetable is not too soft, so that it can hold up against the stew!

Dice the onion, and cook it until translucent. Add the meat (or veggie substitute), and sear it, with the chopped garlic (optional). Once seared, add the tomatoes (optional) and cook for another 2-5 minutes. After, add water, tomato paste, peanut butter, bouillon cubes, thyme (optional) and chili pepper, as well as some white pepper and a touch of salt. Stir until a consistent paste is formed, then cook down on low heat, covered, until the paste is as thick as a stew. Once the stew is ready and thick enough, serve on top of rice, or Jollof rice if you want to make. No matter what, the stew is rich and amazing, ensuring that the rice it is served atop of will never be bland or untasty. You can make the stew even better if you would like, serving it on top of Jollof rice instead of simple white rice!

Jollof rice:
- Rice
- Onion
- Tomato paste
- Garlic (optional)
- Bouillon cubes diluted in water (or just stock in general; will work just fine as well)
- Tomatoes
- Herbs (preferably Thyme and bay leaf)
- White pepper
- Bell peppers
- Oil

Dice the onion, then cook it in a pot until translucent. Add the garlic (optional) and rice, cooking until the rice is golden brown. Then, blend all remaining ingredients, except for the herbs (tomato paste,bell pepper, tomatoes) with a bit of water, and add the blended mixture to the rice, as you would a Jambalaya, and stir. Add the bouillon water to the rice, as well as herbs, and cover.

Simmer on low heat, until all of the water has been absorbed. Remove the bay leaf. The Jollof rice is now ready to be eaten!

It is sometimes nice to simmer a little longer, if enough oil has been added to the rice, achieving a delicious crispy bottom of rice. Don't simmer it for too long, or the exterior part of the rice will absolutely burnt.

This Jollof rice is also incredibly good with some fried chicken on the side; many people believe that there is no need for such a flavorful rice if the stew is already imparting so much flavor.

**Pasta soup, topped with seared chicken**
This may sound crazy, but I came up with this one when in a McDonalds in Macau. For their breakfast menu, they serve pasta soup topped with chicken. I am not joking. This is the first time I have ever even heard of any pasta being served at McDonalds, but hey, Macau proved me wrong after all. The craziest

part was, the dish was actually really good! It is like a spin on the usual chicken noodle soup, which I already enjoy. I will definitely include a recipe for chicken noodle soup, as it is such a cheap and delicious classic. I use Rotini pasta because of its large size, which is usually very filling and does not get mushy too easily, which is very nice for a soup. The best thing to do for this recipe is to serve it in a rather shallow bowl, so that the seared chicken can remain crispy and not too wet. It is also recommended to serve the soup with a bit of bread, toasted or not, to soak up all of that remaining delicious soup at the end. Here is the recipe:

Pasta soup:
- Rotini pasta
- Celery
- Carrot
- Onion
- Salt, pepper
- Bouillon cube
- leeks
- Peas
- Soy beans or soy bean sprouts (optional, but if you have the choice edamame soy beans work very well. Any soy beans will work for this recipe however)
- Chicken breast (for the end, so optional as well)
- Bay leaves (optional)

- Touch of hot sauce (preferably tabasco; optional)

Cook the celery, carrot and onion, as well as leeks (optional) all diced, in a pot, at medium temperature, until the onions are translucent. Add the bouillon cube, and water, as well as the soybeans (optional) and chicken (or other) bones(optional). Cook down for a while, adding salt and pepper if wanted, to taste. Add pasta, and simmer until the pasta is to your liking. Some people like more crunchy pasta, some people like softer pasta. I like mine "al dente", personally.
Put in bowl, and top with perfectly seared/grilled chicken. There you go! An incredible bowl of pasta soup!


**Garlic bread with rubbed tomato**
So simple, yet so delicious… this is more of a snack than a full course, but you can definitely turn it into a full meal by adding some delicious soup with it, like the tomato or the chicken noodle soup! What I love about this dish is that you really don't need much at all: garlic, bread, tomato. Just the same way as the Spanish do it! You can choose to go fancy by sprinkling some cheese and herb on top as well, then putting it in the oven, but the simple version is so simple that all you need is a toaster. SO, I will have

two recipes: the fancy garlic bread and the classic garlic tomato bread

Classic garlic tomato bread:
- Bread (ideally a very flavorful bread, whole grain or something, but as usual any bread will work)
- Garlic
- Tomato
- Herb oil (optional)
- Salt, pepper

Toast the bread. Right when it comes out of the toaster, rub the raw garlic onto it as quickly as you can. The bread is still hot and crunchy and will soak up all of that delicious garlic flavor. Then, cut the tomato in half and rub that onto the bread as well. Top with salt, pepper, and herb oil (optional). Finished! Now how simple and cheap is that, seriously.


**Fancy garlic bread**
If you are having a dinner or a cocktail party, then this incredibly tasty treat could be for you! It is best served with either marinara sauce, or a nice honey dijon mustard (homemade, mix dijon mustard with a bit of honey, that is all. Some people like to add dill to the sauce as well, I personally think it is

unnecessary for this recipe but it is definitely worth trying at least once). Anyways here is the recipe:

<u>Fancy garlic bread:</u>

-Bread

-Butter

-Garlic

-Cheese (any will work, but ideally get some cheese that melts good (cheddar or manchego for example) and top that off with some Parmesan cheese)

-Herbs (optional, ideally parsley, oregano, and/or sage)

Chop the bread into slices. Smear one side with butter.

Add chopped garlic, cheese and chopped herbs to the bread.

Stick the bread into the oven, and broil until the cheese has melted and getting incredibly crispy.

Voila! You have now delicious, scrumptious garlic bread!

Same dipping sauces as before are recommended for this masterpiece. Nobody can never get enough garlic bread, it is just too delicious to be honest with you.

## Chicken noodle soup:

Ahh, the famous chicken noodle soup… so heartwarming, so cheap, and soooo delicious. Everybody remembers when they were sick as children, with the mother always giving a nice bowl of heartwarming chicken noodle soup. To tell you the truth, I have no idea if the chicken noodle soup actually cured my sickness, but I always associate it with better times to come the next day. One thing is sure: chicken noodle soup is definitely not unhealthy. The recipe:

Chicken noodle soup:
-Chicken (carcass, meat and/or bones. One thing is certain: bones will give good flavor to the soup)
-Carrots
-Celery
-Onion
-Salt (celery salt is actually very nice for this)
-Pepper
-Noodles (spaghetti is ideal)
-Other large vegetables, like potato or corn (optional)
-Herbs (optional; ideally fennel, parsley and/or thyme)
-Leeks (optional)

Dice up the carrots, onions, celery, leeks. Cook in a pot at medium heat (preferably a crockpot) until onions are translucent. Add chicken, and cook for a little longer. Then add salt, water and pepper. Add the noodles, and cook until the noodles are ready. Boom! Chicken noodle soup is served. Delicious as always.

The difference here from the other recipe are essentially the whole pieces of chicken which are found in the soup. Chicken noodle soup has more of a chicken flavor, compared to the pasta soup. So, some big chunky pieces of chicken with bone are the norm for chicken noodle soup in my opinion. Keep the bone in, as it will give the chicken noodle soup more of a depth in flavor. This dish is definitely great for leftover chicken, or even chicken carcasses. We want to create as much flavor as possible, as usual. It is important to save as much money as possible, and this dish (soups in general) is a great way to ensure that no food ever goes to waste.

**Pad Thai**
Did you know that Pad Thai was a recipe made up in the 1960's, by the Thai King's chef at the time, as a measure to keep the nation from splitting up? People legitimately got mail at their doorstep, saying: "now you eat Pad Thai, as the national dish!". Making Pad Thai was necessary for the country, as people needed to understand how to make use of the incredible supply of rice noodles that the country was producing. Pad Thai was the most delicious and cheap method they could think of.

     A traditional Pad Thai will use a million different sauces to make Pad Thai sauce, like Tamarind Paste, shrimp paste and some very special soy sauce which is very tricky to find, so I have dumbed down the recipe a tad, making it more easily accessible and cheap. Don't worry, it will still be absolutely delicious!

Finally, this is another one of those dishes which can take a pretty enormous amount of ingredients. It is great at the end of the week when there is some leftover food in the fridge: whether it's chicken, shrimp, or veggies, most of the time leftover food will be appropriate for a Pad Thai! I will put the base of the recipe, and then give many great ideas on what you could add into your pad thai, from last minute garnishes to meats to veggies.

Pad Thai:
base:
- Noodles (ideally flat rice noodles, but honestly most noodles will work for this dish)
- Fish sauce
- Soy sauce
- Chillies
- Lime (ideally, but lemon works too)
-rice wine vinegar (optional)
- Ginger (optional)
- Garlic
- Little bit of brown sugar (palm sugar is ideal, but if you have neither just a bit of normal sugar will work too. Need that little amount of sweetness, basically)
-Teeny bit of oil

Smash the garlic and ginger (optional) with the chillies, and a touch of fish sauce, until obtaining a paste. Heat a hot pan, ideally a wok, with some oil at the bottom. Add the vegetables and meats which will take some time to cook. Once it has cooked, add the garlic ginger paste, followed shortly by the noodles, and cook until perfection.

Mix soy sauce, as well as the sugar, lime zest, lime juice and the rest of the fish sauce, into a bowl, and pour sauce when the noodles are almost done cooking. You want as much flavor as possible in that sauce, so feel free to add more ingredients to it, adding more dimensions to the Pad Thai profile. Finish with garnish. The most important garnish are the peanuts, in my opinion.

Protein ideas:
- Shrimp
- Beef
- Chicken
- Egg
- Tofu
- Pork (not recommended, but possible and tastes very good as well)

Vegetable ideas:
- Julienned onions
- Julienned carrots
- Sliced red cabbage (mainly for color)
- Snow peas

- Broccoli
- Chinese broccoli
- Bamboo shoots
- Split peas (frozen or not)
- Edamame soy beans

Many more vegetable options are possible. I would not recommend anything that could get blistered or mushy, like a tomato. However, a sun dried tomato could be very interesting in a Pad Thai, now that I think about it.

<u>Garnish ideas:</u>
- peanuts (most important!)
- Green onions/scallions
- Cilantro/coriander leaves
- Soybean sprouts
- Touch of sesame oil (seriously optional, some Thai people would kill me for saying this)
- Lime zest
- Lime juice

Overall, I am definitely using a loose term for Pad Thai here. An actual Thai person might try to kill you for calling this dish Pad Thai, but in my opinion it has enough Pad Thai 'flair' for me to call it Pad Thai without too many people rolling their eyes. No matter what, this dish is absolutely delicious!

**Falafel**

Everyone likes falafel; who doesn't? They are fried balls of goodness, so savory and delicious in so many different ways. Best of all, falafel is ridiculously cheap! There is a reason why Falafel is the go-to street food in many Middle Eastern countries: it is cheap AND it is delicious. It's literally just chickpeas (also called garbanzo beans, depends who you ask) blended with some spices and seasonings for flavor, then fried up until golden brown on the outside.
The classic way of eating the falafel would be in pita bread, with some tomato cucumber salad, cabbage, pickles, and of course never forget the lemon tahini sauce! Of course, different countries add different toppings to their falafel. The Egyptian falafel has different toppings compared to the Sudanese falafel or Israeli falafel. There are always more things you can add to your falafel, the most classic ones being fried eggplant, pickled and marinated carrots, coriander and turmeric spiced cauliflower, lettuce, pickled radishes (looks pink usually), fries, and so on. There will be a list make a list of common toppings and accompanying condiments on the bottom. For some reason in Israel AND Lebanon everyone likes putting fries in their Pita bread. I think it's a bit ridiculous but it's at least worth a try.
A big thing is: you don't need pita bread to make this recipe work. Falafel salad is delicious, falafel on top

of rice is delicious (make sure to use seasoned rice and include a sauce though), or even Falafel by itself is absolutely delicious! They are also great because you can make a rather large batch of Falafel dough, which will hold up nicely in the fridge for at least a bit of time before you need to fry them up. You can also freeze the dough, making it last longer. So, it is possible and even recommended to make a big batch of this stuff. You can fry these tasty balls on demand this way, ensuring a healthy, cheap and delicious meal or snack at any time. Anyways here is the recipe:

Falafel:
- Chickpeas (dry chickpeas are ideal, but buying canned WILL work. Just won't be as good as with canned, besides dry chickpeas are waaaaay cheaper if you do the math)
- Little bit of flour
- Cardamom, (ground is ideal, but whole is cheaper so just buy whole and then grind up later)
- Coriander seeds, crushed
- Cumin
- Parsley
- Cilantro (definitely optional, some people like it with but i personally think it's unnecessary)
- Sesame (very optional as well)
- Garlic, minced
- Minced onion

- Salt, pepper

Rehydrate the dried chickpeas. Soak them in water at least overnight and up to 24 hours, with a little bit of salt. Some people but a pinch of baking soda as well, you can do it and it does add volume to the chickpeas but it is not totally necessary at all.

Toast the spices (cumin, coriander seeds and cardamom) then crack them ever so slightly (if they are not already ground up). Add some salt, pepper and the chickpeas into a food processor. Blitz until they have a coarse texture. Then, add the parsley, cilantro, flour, chopped onion and garlic. Blitz a little bit longer, but do not blitz for too long as we don't want our falafel mixture to have too smooth of a texture. Depending on how much parsley and cilantro is added, you can decide to make the falafel mixture green or not.

Make tiny balls using two spoons (there is a cool Falafel spoon specifically designed to make Falafel balls, it is a fun spoon to have but if you are not making these falafel balls everyday then it may not be worth it), cover the balls in sesame seeds (optional) and fry them until golden brown. Your falafel balls should be a little smaller than a golf ball, but again there are no rules to how big or small your balls are supposed to be. Every country has different sized falafel balls, anyways.

Boom! There, you just made scrumptious falafel! Ideally you put it in some pita bread and make a delicious sandwich, but if not pita bread most breads will work fine, as long as the works are in them the falafel sandwich (or salad, or rice or whatever) should indeed be delicious.

The works:
- Bread (ideally pita bread, but any bread will work. Some people have put it in lavash, flour tortilla, or even a toasted burger bun, and said that it was absolutely delicious)
- Diced tomatoes
- Diced cucumber
- Red cabbage, julienned
- Pickles (there is a certain type of pickle which works best, but don't worry about that. Find which type of pickle works best for you)
- Tahini sauce ( just mix tahini (which is sesame paste essentially), water, lemon juice, salt. Blend it until silky smooth, and the sauce is officially ready)
- Spicy green sauce (optional; literally just blend some jalapenos in a food processor with a tiny bit of water and that's it. You can add some cumin for fun, if you would like)

There is always the option of adding more toppings, like fried eggplant or even French fries, but the works is definitely what a falafel needs as accompaniment,

either with or without bread. Some examples of extra toppings:
- Hummus (either homemade (cheaper overall, pg 73) but store bought is fine)
- Fried eggplant
- Pickled and/or marinated carrot slices
- Coriander-marinated cauliflower
- Lettuce
- Greek yogurt (Ideally Labneh, but we have to be realistic here)
- Hard boiled egg
- A bit of bulgur wheat
- Fresh parsley or coriander
- Any topping your mind thinks will taste good with the current combination of ingredients.

Some like to use a fresh squeeze of lemon on their sandwich, I personally do not think that it's necessary. Everyone gets to choose what they want I suppose. Be creative with this sandwich! Many combinations are possible.

If you do not have tahini sauce, I found that a nice garlic aioli (mayo, salt, lemon juice, minced garlic) works extremely well. In Egypt, they use Fava beans instead of chickpeas as the base, so if you have some Fava beans lying around use those instead, or you can even create a blend of different beans that you want to fry. Possibilities are almost endless!

**Chickpea salad**

I like this salad, mainly because of its simplicity. It's also a great way to get rid of any extra garbanzo beans that were cooked and unused.

I love salads in general, because all you really need to do is chop some stuff up, add a nice dressing, and voila! Delicious salad. Pros like putting nuts and cheese into the salad, which I will agree with 99% of the time, but those things can be expensive. So I will show the stripped down cheap salad, and then put the optional ingredients, which are nuts and cheese

Chickpea salad:
- Chickpeas, boiled until they reach about the same firmness as a can of chickpeas (about 1hr if completely dry, maybe 30-40 minutes if already rehydrated). Can also use almost any bean. Fava beans, white beans or even kidney beans are pretty darn good for this! Other beans can also definitely be used, like the versatile black eyed peas
- Cucumber
- Tomato
- Red onion
- Some greens (lettuce, mesclun or other greens. Once I used turnip greens and it was actually pretty darn good! Can also be replaced by chopped parsley)

- Simple vinaigrette dressing (vinegar/lemon, oil, mustard, salt and pepper. I recommend it to be a little bit more acid for this salad, and not too much mustard, but everyone is a free man! As usual, of course)
- Mint, parsley (optional)
- Cheese (optional, but crumbled feta cheese is recommended)
- Nuts (optional, but sunflower seeds are recommended as they are cheap nuts)
- Homemade croutons (optional)

Cube the cucumber and tomato, then slice the red onion as thinly as you can, ideally using a mandolin. You can also choose to mince the onion, if you would like. We just don't want the salad to have too much of a raw red onion flavor. Throw the greens (chopped if needed), as well as the mint and parsley, chopped. Then, add the simple vinaigrette dressing, and toss everything up. FInish with some salt, pepper, nuts and cheese. We do not mix the nuts, cheese and croutons with the dressing in order to keep them from breaking and bruising up.

Enjoy this simple yet delicious dish! I really love how filling this salad is, with the chickpeas just filling you up. It's a great thing to eat on the go, as long as you keep the dressing on the side. A big bowl of chickpea salad is more than enough for lunch for me, which is pretty awesome actually.

**Peanut butter noodles**

I have been focusing on peanuts and peanut butter quite a bit, mainly because peanut butter is seriously cheap and can be used in a wide variety of applications. Like peanut butter noodles! They are seriously simple and seriously delicious. I remember the first time I had these noodles like if it was yesterday: I was very young, camping in New Hampshire I believe. When camping, you cannot bring anything that could spoil. Mainly, you are subject to dried food, canned food, and other condiments which do not spoil fast. Such items, without a doubt, are a jar of peanut butter and a bag of spaghetti noodles. Making the peanut butter sauce and watching it coat all of those noodles in such a uniform manner, truly magical.

Here, we are not camping so I can add some fun garnishes. As usual, we are cooking for cheap so it is understandable and ok if you remove the garnishes. I will add a few, just for fun, but seriously absolutely none are necessary

Peanut butter noodles:
- Peanut butter
- Ginger
- Garlic (optional)
- Rice wine vinegar (can also use lemon juice/lime juice (at that point use the zest too),

- and/or white wine vinegar. Sherry wine vinegar can give a nice touch)
- Hot peppers (optional, but I highly recommend)
- Soy sauce
- Tablespoon of sugar (ONLY if the peanut butter you are using has no sugar in it already)
- Salt, pepper
- Noodles

Heat a pot of water, adding salt to it. Put the noodles in.

Meanwhile, mince the ginger and hot pepper very finely (removing the seeds for the hot pepper), and cook them in a pan. Add minced/crushed garlic (optional), as well as rice wine vinegar, peanut butter, soy sauce, and pasta water. Cook at simmering temperatures, adding salt, pepper and pasta/noodle water as necessary. Sometimes the sauce gets too thick, and pasta/noodle water has more flavor than normal water. This is a super neat trick!

Once the noodles are cooked, drain them and stick them directly into that amazing peanut sauce. Coat well, and garnish. Remember, all garnishes are optional! The peanut butter noodles are totally delicious without.

Garnish ideas:
- Scallions, chopped
- Coriander, chopped
- Fried garlic

- Touch of sesame oil
- Sesame seeds

**Popcorn**
This might sound strange, but I am not joking when I am saying that popcorn is one of the cheapest things you can buy. You must buy the popcorn kernels themselves, not the popcorn bag. And one bag of popcorn kernels can make a whole ton of popcorn. Think about it: one half cup of popcorn kernels will turn into a huge bowl of popcorn, more than I can even eat! So one 3 dollar bag of popcorn kernels can seriously last several months.

The best way to pop corn in my opinion is to use that air popper machine. You just plug it into the wall, and hot air will pop the corn. I think this is my preferred method because there is not even a need to use any oil or anything, saving money in the process. Of course, however, drizzling some melted butter or drizzling a tiny bit of oil at the end will help the salt added to stick to the popcorn, which is why I usually recommend some oil or something at the end. However, if you don't have/don't want to use oil then it's totally fine, the salt may end up at the bottom of the bowl but you will be eating some good popcorn regardless.

There are many things you can do to popcorn. Loaded popcorn is one of my favorite all-time things, but there are also popcorn cakes and treats that can be made as well. Did you know that popcorn is routinely added to soups as a crouton replacement/thickener in Ecuador? We will explore the depths of what can be made with popcorn, its limits, and my favorite loaded popcorn options.

**Loaded popcorn**

It's very simple, as it is just popcorn covered in different spices/seasonings. Pop some corn, ideally in the air popper machine but if not put some oil into a pan and heat it up to medium-high heat before adding the popcorn kernels and covering the pan, shaking periodically. Once you hear a good amount of kernels popping, be sure to shake the pan up and down constantly. Once you stop hearing pops, the popcorn is ready!

Once the corn is popped and hot, add some butter (ideally melted; if not, you have a hot pan from popping the corn so just use that and melt the butter real quick) to the popcorn, ensuring that the seasonings added will stick to the popcorn. I will include below some of my favorite loaded popcorn options. If you are really broke, some oil will work but will definitely not taste as good. If you are going this route, it may be best to spray the oil on the popcorn, covering it fully without adding too much oil.

Some loaded popcorn ideas are definitely outside of the box and will make some of the popcorn soggy and messy, like the sriracha hot sauce on top of the popcorn. Still absolutely delicious! I will still recommend sriracha popcorn until the day I die.

Loaded popcorn ideas:
- Sriracha (ideally sriracha seasoning, which is a thing. If not the sauce will work fine), chopped cilantro, salt
- Grated parmesan or white cheddar, chopped parsley (no need for salt as cheese itself is fairly salty), pepper
- Curry, Turmeric, salt
- Vinegar flakes, celery salt, pepper
- Ramen noodle seasoning packet
- Sugar, salt
- Caramel, salt (I love sweet and salty, I really do)
- Paprika, salt
- Lime zest, cilantro (or parsley), salt
- Chocolate, chili (whole or flakes)
- Salt, pepper and/or chili flakes
- Cumin, turmeric, ground cardamom

These are just some creative ideas of what you can do with popcorn. You can always make your own combination. Be creative!


**Make your own bread**

This can be cheaper than buying bread! Just be careful on your oven bill for this one.

All you need for bread is yeast, flour, and salt. It's incredibly easy, but the flour you use will have a significant impact on the quality and taste of your bread. The yeast too. It is best to use neither too much or too little yeast. Some people add some sugar in their bread (which is the case with bagels and certain sweetbreads) but I am definitely more of a savory guy, I like sticking to salt.

We will be exploring three different types of bread: flatbread, chapati bread and finally focaccia. For fun, we can also make some bagels. The only reason why I don't really recommend making bagels is that they take a while to make, need a lot of attention, and overall will just not taste as good as many professional bagel shops. This is especially true for the New York and New Jersey people out there: you guys have incredibly good bagels, I tells ya, so don't expect your homemade bagels to compete with the pros of the bagel art.

## Chapati

When you are most broke, this dish WILL save you from total and utter starvation. All you need is flour and water to make a chapati. It is seriously and absolutely that simple. Ideally, use whole grain flour, as it is better for you and has more flavor.

HOWEVER, the Chapati does taste better with some

things one it: butter, herbs, salt, yogurt, some roasted vegetables that can be scooped... Chapati after all is just bread, albeit incredibly cheap bread that can be made pretty darn fast it is still just bread. Nothing more, nothing less. So ideally, definitely eat this chapati with something, it is not means to be alone. The cheapest recommendation I can give is to make some Daal, which is just boiled lentils with a lot of spices. I personally don't know which spices are best, so go to your Indian friends for help on this one. They are usually very nice and have all kinds of spices they put on their Daal, so just ask if you can take a bit of the spices for home, and a majority of them will be more than happy to help you!

Chapati:
- Flour
- Water
- Salt
- Some stuff to put on top of the chapati, or served alongside the Chapati (optional)

Mix flour and water, with a bit of salt, until formation of a dough. On a floured surface, roll out the dough to as thin as you can.

Heat up a pan, medium heat. Put the rolled dough into the pan, pressing it as hard as possible and as often as you can on every inch of the surface. Use a try rag to accomplish this. You want to start seeing the dough to puff. Once the dough puffs, you can flip it for a little more color on the other side. We want an airy, puffy Chapati, not a cracker crust! Too hot, it will burn, too cold it won't puff. So the hardest part is ensuring that your pan is truly nonstick and that the pan is the ideal temperature. Done right, Chapati is absolutely amazing, especially alongside some Daal or other possible dips it can go into.

Serve the Chapati, alongside whatever you have. Some ideas:

- Yogurt + lemon and pepper (touch of salt)
- Garlic and butter (with parsley is very nice too)
- Alongside Daal (a type of lentil which is very popular in India)
- Alongside eggplant stew
- Alongside spinach salad
- Alongside any dressed salad
- Alongside hummus
- Alongside any dip really. Cream cheese and chives is delicious too
- Alongside a nice delicious curry dish. Could be Thai curry, could be Indian curry, could be Nepali curry. In my opinion it really does not matter, to be honest

**Flatbread**

A flatbread is very similar to Chapati, but whereas Chapati is light and really puffs up beautifully, the flatbread is a little bit thicker and a little bit denser, going well with heavier ingredients, very similar to greek pita bread. Its heaviness is great for spearing some spreads (the same as on the chapati), or even adding salad-like ingredients to the top of the flatbread, in order to make it a full meal.

But, essentially, the same sauces and dips that apply to Chapati can apply very well to flatbread. Flatbread is also a little bit more expensive to make, as we are using yogurt instead of water to activate the flour

Flatbread:
- Flour
- Yogurt
- Teeny bit of water if you don't want to use too much yogurt
- Salt, pepper
- Herbs (green onion/ scallions work very well in the dough, in my opinion. Chives as well, but that stuff is expensive)

Mix everything up, until formation of a dough. Work the dough for about 5 minutes, in order to activate the gluten. Then, roll middle finger thick portions of flatbread. Cook on the pan, medium high heat, with no oil or anything in the pan. Cook until both sides have an incredible golden brown color.

Serve with whatever toppings you would like, best ideas being the same as Chapati, essentially (pg.65). Since the bread is thicker, you can definitely have a heavier sauce than Chapati, which can be nice. Pizza, anybody?

## Focaccia

Focaccia is an incredibly simple Italian bread. I like it a lot because you don't need to knead the dough at all, making it one of the quicker and faster bread recipes out there. Focaccia is usually best with rosemary and coarse salt on top of it, but feel free to use as many toppings as you want over it. Some people add olives, some people make a type of focaccia pizza thing. Regardless, focaccia can be incredibly tasty bread. The secret is to knead the dough as little as possible, ensuring a nice spongy bread. The recipe:

Focaccia:
- Flour
- Yeast
- Salt
- Olive oil (or any oil, if you are poor)
- Toppings (none or many; the classic toppings are coarse salt and rosemary)

Mix the flour with the yeast and salt before adding water. You want to mix the flour with the water until the formation of a shaggy dough. You need to knead the dough as little as possible, ensuring a nice fluffy dough. Stick the dough in a bowl which has been covered in olive oil, and let rest with a damp cloth for at least 2 hours. Then, remove the dough from the bowl and knead for maybe a minute. Stick the dough in an oiled baking tray, and let rest with a damp cloth for at least another 30 minutes. Oil the top of the focaccia, put those nubs on the top of the dough with your hands, and add the toppings. Stick in the oven at 220C (425 F, or basically about as hot as your oven goes for most ovens) for 20-30 minutes, until the formation of an amazing golden brown crust. Boom! The focaccia is ready! Making this at home instead of buying it is definitely cheaper, plus you barely need to knead the dough meaning that it takes little effort overall to make focaccia.

**Shakshuka**

One of the easiest (and most delicious) Sunday meals you can cook up, which is incredibly cheap as well! Shakshuka is a fancy work for just spicy tomato sauce with a couple of eggs cracked in the pan, cooked to perfection. Think about a perfectly fried egg surrounded by amazing flavorful spicy tomato sauce. That is exactly what this recipe is all about. It is truly a North African dish, but for some reason everyone in Israel eats this stuff and really loves it.

Harissa can be found in many arabic specialty shops, or online. It is some spicy paste you can put on things. It is different from hot sauce in the sense that it is a paste and not a sauce, and also in the sense that it contains no vinegar, being truly just crushed hot peppers made into a paste that fits in a tube. Feel free to replace the harissa with hot sauce (ideally one with little to no vinegar) or make your own harissa by just blending a large amount of hot peppers in a food processor, with some water, oil and garlic. You can also use a mortar and pestle, if you like.

Anyways, here is the recipe:
<u>Shakshuka:</u>
- Eggs
- Tomatoes, chopped (a can of tomatoes works great for this, even tomato sauce)
- Garlic
- Onion
- Cumin seeds, coriander seeds. If you don't have these then some sort of fragrant spice will work (curry included). Once I used Soy Sauce to replace this ingredient and it worked absolutely fine overall
- Thyme (optional, but an herb in general as a topping is a terrific idea. If no thyme, you can use oregano, sage or bay leaves (pull out the bay leaves before adding toppings and serving) which will work well as a replacement)
- Hot peppers
- Bell peppers (very optional)

- Cheese (as a topping at the end, so optional as well. Ideally parmesan cheese)
- Salt, pepper
- Parsley or cilantro (as a topping)
- Harissa (optional, and truly only if you like spicy things)

Toast some cumin and coriander seeds, then smash them/grind them up. Chop onion and cook in a pan with the hot peppers (and optionally bell peppers), until the onion is translucent. Add garlic and toasted spices, and cook for another minute or two. Add the tomato, and cook down for about 15 minutes. Add salt and pepper, with some harissa if you want to make it spicier after tasting it then make a couple of holes in the sauce. Crack the eggs into the holes, then let simmer, until the eggs are perfectly cooked sunny side up eggs. You can cover the pan during this process, as the steam helps accelerate the cooking of the egg whites. Top with chopped parsley or Cilantro (optional), and cheese (optional), before serving the entire dish in the pan itself.

I like this recipe because since you eat out of the pan, it creates almost no dishes you need to clean up later. For a long time during college, I lived by the rule: one cup, one plate, one pot, one pan, one baking tray, one fork, one spoon, one knife. This was very useful, mainly because even if all of my dishes were dirty in the sink, I would never need to clean up more than that.

**Cracker crusted fish**
This is a very versatile and cheap recipe. I say to crust the fish with crackers, because crackers can be found for free in many places. The is definitely somewhere on your campus which offers free oyster crackers, or a tea place with crackers. Due to the low price of crackers (free!), this makes them the perfect crust element on a fish crust. Recipe:
- Fish
- Crackers
- Garlic (optional)
- 1 jalapeno (optional)
- Herbs (ideally parsley; dried or fresh)

Lemon and butter (for a lemon butter sauce if wanted, but other sauces are possible)

Make the crust. Crack up the crackers in either a blender, food processor, or even by hand. It all depends on how chunky or not you want your cracker crust to be. Mix the crackers with the herbs (dried or not) minced garlic (optional) and sliced jalapeno (optional). Add salt and pepper, until the mixture is absolutely delicious. You can toast this mixture in the oven or in a pan with a teeny bit of oil, if crunch is your thing.

Cook the fish. In a high heat skillet, sear that fish before sticking it in the oven with the crust mixture on top. No need for egg or flour, because the moistness of the fish should be enough for the crust to stick on the fish.

Serve with lemon butter: to make lemon butter keep the pan drippings and mix into them lemon and butter, little by little, until a sauce forms. The butter needs to be cold for an extra foamy sauce. Adding a dollop of creme fraiche helps the sauce's consistency quite a bit, as well.

**Sole meuniere**

Ok, I am not going to lie for this one: sole can be seriously expensive depending on where you live in the world. But somehow in Boston sometimes it is surprisingly cheap. Only maybe one or two dollars more than the cheapest fish there. And trust me, a good sole beats almost anything in this planet. Some restaurants in Paris charge 40 euros for a Sole Meuniere, using the exact same recipe as the one provided. It's literally just a delicious lemon butter sauce poured over a lightly floured perfectly cooked fish. It is a great recipe for a date, served with simple white rice and some veggies, like green beans or peas or anything green really. What is cool about this recipe is that you don't have to use sole; just call it "sole meuniere style" in order to impress your date and serve them an incredible 5 star meal for cheap! Sole Meuniere:

- Whole fish (preferably flat, like sole. Flounder works real nice as well. If you can't get a whole fish, then fillets of fish will work just fine, but a whole fish really does taste better)
- Flour
- Lemon
- Butter
- Parsley (+ tarragon if you can; optional)
- Salt, pepper

Season the flour by adding some salt and pepper to it. Keep the flour seasoning simple, you really want the flavor of the fish to come out.

Cover the fish in the seasoned flour, and cook it in butter until perfectly cooked and golden brown on the outside. While the fish is cooking, chop up the parsley and zest the lemon. That will be for the sauce later.

When the fish is perfect, remove it just 30 seconds before it is perfect, because the hot butter sauce will slightly cook the fish. Keep the pan with all of those fish drippings, and add to it some lemon juice and zest, butter, parsley and tarragon (optional). You will have this unctuous colorful lemon butter sauce, which you can soak the fish in. Voila! Delicious "sole meuniere" for you! This is yet another proof that cooking can limit itself to only a few ingredients, as long as you are able to unlock the full potential of each end every ingredient used. This is how a college student successfully cooks with no waste!

**Fish cakes**

Whenever someone thinks about fish cakes, their first thought is always salmon cake or crab cake. Maybe a tuna cake. No matter what, it's expensive fish. But did you know that you can make an incredibly tasty fish cake without those expensive ingredients? It all comes down to what is put with the fish, baby!
I will show an incredibly simple recipe, with which layers of flavor can be added either into the cakes or on top of the fish cakes. The recipe:

Fish cakes:
- Fish (any fish will do, but since using cheap fish will work just fine in this case just stick to cheap fish or those fake crab sticks. Cans of tuna work great for this dish too!)
- Breadcrumbs (ideally panko or crushed crackers. I LOVE crushed crackers for fish cakes. Even better are those oyster cracker packets, which are technically free)
- Mayonnaise or egg. Egg is cheaper but mayo makes for a much lighter fish cake
- Seasonings
- 1 onion

Mince the onion and sweat it in a pan. Add some salt and pepper. Cut the fish into small pieces. Mix the fish with the onions and breadcrumbs, as well as the mayo, until you can form some fish cakes. You can also add some seasoning at this stage, if desired. Cook the fish cakes on a pan, until a great golden brown color is formed on both sides.

Serve, ideally with some type of remoulade (pg 26).

**Making stock**
Making stock or broth at home is in my opinion is very important. Is is rather simple, just takes a while to cook, and delivers incredible flavor. You can freeze it in containers, to use at any moment when needed. You can make so much with stock, like gravies, soups, and sauces. Basically, it is always good to have some good stock laying around. I will show 3 stock recipes which are all absolute winners: one veggie stock, one meat stock, and finally one fish stock.

I will need to address what a "bouquet garni" is before starting: it is a bunch of herbs wrapped in a string, so that the herbs can easily be removed once the stock is ready.

Most importantly, making stock is one of the best things you can do with vegetable scraps. Just add some onion, carrots and celery, and then all of you veggie scraps can be transformed into a rich flavorful stock.

The veggie stock is the base for all other stocks, so i will address that one first:

Veggie stock:
- Veggie scraps
- Onion
- Carrots
- Celery
- 1 clove of garlic
- 1 "bouquet garni" (optional ; mine will be mainly bay leaves and a couple of sprigs of thyme. Sage is pretty amazing as well)
- Other vegetables, if you would like. I would recommend some dry mushrooms, and even though they will end up making mushroom stock, there is nothing wrong with that!

Cut the onions in half and leave the skins on. Chop the carrots roughly, leaving skin on, as well as the celery. Char the onion halves directly on the stovetop. Most of you will have electric or gas, so this technique will work absolutely fine. If not, charring the onion in a pan works just fine as well.

Then, put all vegetables into a large pot, and add water and salt. If you have a "bouquet garni", this would be the time to put it into the stock pot. Simmer for 3-4 hours, covering the pan most of the way. If you have a pressure cooker the amount of time necessary to make the stock can be reduced to only 2 hours.

The longer the stock is on, the richer it gets, so it is definitely worth waiting. Once ready, you need to strain the stock, leaving only a clear broth. This broth can be portioned and frozen, ready to use for anytime in the year. Many dishes will want some vegetable broth, from soups to making sauces, so having some of this in your freezer at all times is always nice.

Meat stock:

To get a meat carcass, it is actually a lot easier than everyone thinks. When you roast a whole chicken, be sure to keep the bones, as you can use that for stock later. Also, some butchers sell meat bones at ridiculously cheap prices. If you cannot find any meat carcasses, then the cheapest meat cuts should work fine as well.

Meat stock (chicken or beef being the most famous ones; do not mix them!):
- Everything that is in the veggie stock
- Meat carcass

Brown the meat carcasses in the oven, cooking them for about 1 hour in order for them to release their flavors more. Then stick them with all of the veggie stock components, reducing for about 3-4 hours. Done!

Fish stock:
This is best with fish bones; I once made a delicious fish stock using crab shells as my base, to which I added some fennel, onions, celery and carrots. Fish stock is meant to be lighter, so no need for so many vegetables for this fish stock

Fish stock:
- Fennel
- Onion
- Fish scraps
- "Bouquet garni" (optional)

That is all! Put everything into a pot and simmer, just like before. Fish stock is the greatest base for making fish bisque down the line, which is also absolutely delicious


**Tuna salad**
Why is tuna so cheap? Seriously, the cheapest can of tuna can be pretty filling, and it is only 89 cents! In Costco that price drops dramatically. Having tuna on its own is not super amazing, but a great tuna salad is. We are looking for the cheapest, most delicious tuna salad which needs to be incredibly cheap, and that means of course mixing the tuna with some breadcrumbs in order to stretch it a little bit.

Tuna salad does not need to be complicated, but it must be packed with flavor. This recipe is definitely packed with flavor. I would ideally want to add some capers to this, but that is expensive so I will be skipping the capers all together. However, if you are feeling rich and adventurous then please, add some chopped up capers to this tuna salad!

<u>Tuna salad:</u>
- Can of tuna
- Celery
- Onion
- Garlic (optional)
- Mayonnaise
- Paprika (optional)
- Parsley (optional but recommended)
- Pickles, and the pickling brine as well
- Breadcrumbs (any type works, but if there is choice the cracked crackers work well)
- Salt, pepper

Mince onion and garlic ; dice pickles and celery. Mix with tuna, breadcrumbs, mayonnaise, a little bit of pickle juice, salt and pepper. Boom! Delicious tuna salad. Goes great on toast, and is very filling. Seriously a great dish in my opinion.

## Hummus

Hummus, hummus, hummus…Everyone loves hummus! And what is there not to love about it? It is a delicious bean spread! Now, to be 100% honest, the cheapest way of making hummus is to speak to HIllel and make them throw a hummus making event on campus. That way, you get everything paid for, and can even bring a bunch of Hummus home! That's the way I got so much tahini in my place: it was all donated to me from Hillel!

Hummus:
- Chickpeas (dried, soaked overnight with ideally a bit of baking soda)
- Garlic
- Lemon juice
- Tahini
- Olive oil (really as a topping so optional)
- Smoked paprika (as a topping, so optional)
- Cumin (just a pinch, and it's completely optional)
- Salt

Boil the chickpeas with some salt for 1-2 hours. It really depends on the chickpeas, and this sounds crazy but they have to 'feel' right: not too soft and not too firm. Basically if you can squeeze the chickpea between the finger and thumb, and the chickpea smushes effortlessly, then you are on the right track.

Do not drain the chickpeas! The cooking liquid is super duper precious and important! Also, it has a lot of nutrients and is great for sauces and soups and stuff.

Put the still hot chickpeas into a food processor, with the garlic, lemon juice, tahini, salt and chickpea cooking liquid. Blitz until silky smooth. Remember, you can always add more chickpea water for a smoother result!

The secret to great hummus is simply the perfect balance of all 4 main ingredients: chickpeas, garlic, lemon juice, a bit of olive oil (optional) and tahini. So taste often, salt as necessary, and taste until you are happy with your hummus result. Serve, with some olive oil drizzled on top and a bit of smoked paprika. Hummus goes great on basically anything, so you know it will be a delicious time!

**Stuffed anything**
It is incredible to stuff some foods with other foods! Stuffed turkey, stuffed chicken, stuffed cucumber, stuffed eggplant, stuffed pumpkin or squash… possibilities are limitless! This is a great way to utilize some leftover ingredients and put them into stuffing in order to waste the least amount of food

possible. I will provide examples of two ingredients that can be stuffed, but remember, anything can be stuffed! Once I stuffed this garlic herb mixture into burger patties, so that each bite can have some serious oomph of flavor. Stuffing burger patties with some cheese is a classic, too. Anyways, when going to the farmers market you can always think: can i stuff this?

**Stuffed tomatoes/zucchini**

There is almost nothing cheaper out there! And a stuffed tomato is so cool and sexy, too. You just empty the pulp of a tomato, fill it with anything you want, pop that sucker in the oven and voila! Delicious stuffed tomatoes. Even sexier if you keep the head of the tomato, to make some type of hat. This is a great way to make people eat veggies, in general.
I will provide two different stuffing ideas for the tomato, but remember that you can stuff the tomato with whatever you want. Seriously! Just make sure that everything the stuffing would make sense nestled inside a tomato. Be sure to use the tomato pulp that gets cored out! You don't have to use it in the stuffing like I do, but regardless all parts of any food can have some use and are worth keeping.

Stuffed tomatoes:
- Fresh tomatoes, whole. Ideally larger tomatoes, as you can fit more stuffing in there

- Stuffing (will provide two examples below) or egg
- Chopped herbs (optional)

Slice the top of the tomato. Set aside.
Using a spoon, carefully remove the pulp of the tomato, while still keeping the skin intact. You can keep the tomato pulp and do a million different things with it,.
Fill the tomato with the appropriate stuffing or egg
Put the tomato in the oven at high heat, until the ingredients are cooked.
Remove the tomatoes from the oven, and add some chopped herbs (optional), and place the "hat" on top of the tomatoes. Serve, typically alongside some rice and sometimes salad.

Vegetable only stuffing:
- Zucchini
- Breadcrumbs
- Chopped herbs (ideally parsley, but optional of course)
- Onion
- Garlic
- Squash (or any other vegetable laying around. Even potato would be delicious!
- Tomato pulp (gotten from the tomato core)
- White wine (optional)

- Spices (optional; curry actually works really well for this recipe!)
- Rice, cooked

Cube the zucchini and squash, and mince the onions and garlic. Sweat the onions first, then add the garlic. Add the tomato pulp, with the zucchini and squash. Cook for a bit then add the white wine (optional), salt, pepper and spices (optional). Finish with chopped herbs and rice. The stuffing is now ready to go inside the tomato! Add the breadcrumbs on top of the filled tomato, in order to achieve more of a crunch to the tomato.

Meat stuffing (a bit more expensive):
Essentially, it's a meatball stuffed in a tomato! Absolutely delicious. As usual, you can replace the meat with some beans, or some meat other than ground beef:
- Ground beef
- Garlic
- Onion
- Capers( optional)
- Parmesan cheese (optional)
- Olives (optional)
- Herbs (ideally parsley and oregano. Optional of course)

- Breadcrumbs, toasted if desired for extra flavor
- Egg

Chop everything very finely (garlic, onion, capers (optional), olives (optional), herbs). Mix into the ground beef with breadcrumbs, parmesan (optional), egg, as well as salt and pepper. Stuffing is complete! It is ready to go directly inside the tomato, as the meat will cook in the oven with the tomato.

**Make a salad out of anything**

I think that is is an important skill to know how to turn anything into a salad. What is a salad, anyways? It is just a bunch of random stuff mixed in a bowl! You can add croutons, nuts, raisins, veggies, fish, meat, and more to your salad, there are seriously no rules. Again, making a salad is a good way to use your leftovers at the end of the week. Just make sure that the salad dressing is appropriate with whatever you are making. For a cobb salad, it is usually a thick yogurt or mayo dressing. For a light salad, it is usually a simple vinaigrette drizzled onto some greens. No matter what, my favorite salad is the chopped salad. Just chop up all of your ingredients really fine, add some dressing to bind it all together, and boom! Amazing chopped salad!

I don't think that there is a need to make a 'anything salad' recipe, but I do think it would be nice to share with you some of my favorite salad dressings. They are super simple to make, and truly give an oomph to any salad.

Also, if you decide to go fancy, the best things to add in a salad are nuts and herbs and cheese and stuff! All nuts and almost all cheeses will work in some types of salad, I guarantee it :) you can also make your own croutons for an extra crunch in the salad! To

Dressing ideas:
- Simple vinaigrette: vinegar (or lemon or lime juice) ⅓ and oil 2/3 . Fancy oils work really nice, or some of those cool herb or chili oils we made previously as well.
- Asian vinaigrette: soy sauce, honey, rice wine vinegar (or lime), sesame oil (can replace with any oil if you don't have that, but sesame oil is definitely best)
- French vinaigrette: vinegar, oil, mustard. The sauce can get quite thick once properly blended
- Yogurt vinaigrette: yogurt, oil, acid (any kind, depends on the flavor you want, but lemon juice is best), herbs, minced garlic (optional, but I am a garlic lover and)

- Honey mustard dressing: honey, mustard, oil, vinegar, salt, pepper
- Caesar dressing (by far the most expensive dressing on the list, but my personal favorite. This is not DRD budget dressing I will not lie): Anchovies, capers, olive oil, lemon juice, parmesan, 1 clove chopped garlic, some Dijon mustard, worcestershire sauce, an egg yolk, salt and pepper
-  Garlic-ginger dressing: chopped garlic, grated ginger, soy sauce, honey (or sugar if poor), one hot chili, lemon juice (or rice wine vinegar), oil (ideally sesame oil)
- Mayo dressing (aioli): mayo, lemon juice, garlic, salt, pepper, herbs and chili if you like. Simple aioli should definitely be thinner than mayo, but sooo delicious coating the whole salad
- Pesto dressing: nuts (any, ideally pine nuts but so expensive so even sunflower seeds are nice), basil, garlic, lemon juice, cheese (ideally parmesan), olive oil (or one of those flavored oils), salt and pepper

**Pizza salad**

As a college student going to all of these clubs and activities, there will be a lot of opportunities to bring back a box of leftover pizza. I have many memories of clubs which planned for a much larger event than actually necessary, resulting in sometimes whole pizza boxes being leftover from the event. Make sure to bring that box of pizza home! There are many ways to transform pizza into something other than pizza, such as pizza salad, pizza panini, and pizza soup. Pizza is just bread sauce and cheese, so it is great used as a sauce thickener, croutons or other amazing purposes. We will explore all of these versatile options.

Pizza salad:
- Leftover pizza
- Lettuce, or any type of salad greens. cabbage works great as well
- Light dressing. The simplest is just some French vinaigrette (recipe above), but just lemon juice and oil is also delicious. This recipe also goes incredibly well with mayonnaise based dressings, such as a simple garlic aioli dressing (garlic, mayo, lemon juice, salt)

Make some pizza croutons: Separate the cheese from the pizza. We will be frying this cheese later, for extra crispiness to the salad. Cut the pizza into small cubes or strips and fry it in a nonstick pan with a teeny bit of oil, until the pizza bits become crispy and delicious. Remove the pizza croutons and add the

cheese to the pan, cooking it on medium-low heat until you get some cheese crisps.
Chop the salad and toss it with the dressing and pizza croutons, as well as crispy cheese bits.
serve.
And that's it! delicious pizza salad cooked up and served in no time.


**Pizza panini**

I made this recipe a lot whenever I got sick of the dining hall food. The only annoying part about this recipe is that ideally a panini press is used. if you don't have a panini press, a waffle iron works great as well (they have one in my dining hall). Last resort, press the pizza panini on a hot oiled pan with a spatula: this will help keep it down and get some nice color on each side of the pizza panini.

<u>Pizza panini:</u>
- 2 slices of pizza
- Panini stuff. a classic combination is ham and cheese, or spinach and cheese, but I like to put tomatoes, onions, and spinach in mine. There is a really good one with goat cheese and herbs, but that's expensive. The cheapest options would be tomato and mozzarella, or grilled vegetables such as eggplant and

zucchini or even squash and raisins. Basically go to a panini shop for inspiration on what to put inside your pizza-nini.

Fill as much panini filling as you can between 2 slices of pizza. stick it in a hot oiled panini press and cook until both sides are crispy and the sandwich is properly flattened. Serve.
This dish might be a bit messy, but oh man is it delicious!

## PASTA SALAD

Pasta salad is so delicious! Very few people think about how yummy cold pasta dishes can actually be. Most importantly, this may be the best way to use leftover pasta! Even if the pasta has some tomato sauce or other sauce on it, it is still possible to make decent pasta salad.
This may sound crazy, but the pasta salads usually taste better when using leftover pasta. It may have to do with the fact that we are giving time for the pasta to absorb its surrounding oils. Anyways, here is the recipe:
Pasta salad:
- Pasta, cooked (ideally leftover pasta, to be honest. For some reason it tastes better for this recipe)
- Pesto (or a light vinaigrette works as well)

- Tomatoes, cubed (or cherry tomatoes)
- Cheese
- Breadcrumbs
- Vegetables, chopped
- Herbs (optional)

Mix everything in a bowl, until the ingredients all get to know each other. Add salt and pepper to taste.

As you can tell, pasta salad is ridiculously simple! It's like making salad, but instead of lettuce, we have pasta! I will be honest that in my opinion, this recipe works best with penne pasta, but butterfly or even spaghetti will be fine. Although personally I would re-fry spaghetti in the pan, very similar to the way I would stir fry noodles, before making the salad. To each their own!

**Potato filled chapati with spread/dip**
Now, I will admit that this is frozen food, meaning that if you made it yourself, you would be saving quite a bit of money. However, for this it is okay because frozen chapati is very cheap for what it is. I got 15 chapati for about 7 dollars and can safely say that they save my life as a late night snack. Make sure it is potato filled, as it is more filling for your stomach compared to other filled chapatis you can buy. I like these Chapati as an emergency: if I get home late and don't have the time or the energy to cook, then this

incredibly fast and tasty frozen treat will save my life. I usually eat Chapati around 2 or 3 am, when I just want to eat and then pass out.

What is incredible about Chapati is its versatility. Almost any spread or dip can go on it! Which is why I am keeping the recipe very open-ended.

Chapati:
-chapati (homemade or frozen)
-dips, toppings

Cook the chapati on a pan with no oil, on high heat, until you get some char on both sides. Remove from pan, place on a plate, and add some toppings or dip while it is still hot. Serve as a pizza, sliced, or as a taco, folded in half.

My favorite dip combos are:
- Butter and cheese
- Peanut butter and jelly
- Horseradish and herbs
- Roasted onions and garlic
- Boursin cheese (expensive but you know, if you have it available at a cocktail party...)
- Cream cheese and chives/green onion
- Yogurt and olive oil

But, as everything, experiment and find your personal favorite dip! You will not regret having these in your freezer at all times trust me :)

If you want to make this flaky chapati yourself, just wrap Indian style cooked potatoes into some chapati dough. It's that simple.

Remember, you can stuff the chapati with whatever you want! Spinach and cheese never tastes bad in my opinion, especially with spices like cardamom and sumac or cumin. Just make sure to never overspice any dish!

**Huevos rancheros**

This literally translates to "ranger eggs". No matter what the name is, this is a way to extend the calories + nutrients of your eggs for a cheap price. the lesson from this recipe should be: "put some stuff into your eggs! it's worth it :)".

Of course, as I understand that this is budget cooking, most people will cook this with only eggs. but it's still good to know that eggs can be so much more.

Huevos rancheros:
- Egg
- Tomato
- Cumin
- Onions (optional)
- Garlic (optional)
- Hot peppers (like habaneros if you are crazy or jalapenos if you are a normal person)

- Lime (optional)

Dice the onion, tomato, jalapeno (optional) and garlic. thick garlic, well toasted, is amazing for this recipe. throw all diced ingredients in a hot pan, and once they are properly browned add the eggs. cook until your eggs preference. I personally like my eggs wet. serve, ideally with salt, pepper and lime.
a delicious cheap local Mexican dish was created! this is yet again proof that the tastiest dishes come from poverty. with poverty, you make the most out of every ingredient used, which is simply amazing:)

**Leblebi (the Tunisian-style)**

Ahh, leblebi… it is so simple, yet so satisfying! A very typical Tunisian breakfast. I fell in love with it during my trip in Tunisia, it was just the best stew you can ask for on a hot sunny day. It is especially great to make when you have old bread, as this dish can repurpose it perfectly. This dish normally is every ingredient Tunisia offers in the same bowl: baguette, tabel spice mix, tuna, olives, harissa and chickpeas topped with an egg. Obviously, ideally if you are in Tunisia then you can get harissa and tabel spice mix for cheap, as well as tuna and olives. In other countries, not so easy. However, the idea of putting a hot chickpea stew on top of shredded bread is a great one, and even though this homemade leblebi may not taste as good as the one in Tunisia it is still absolutely worth trying and enjoying many times. The greatest advantage of this dish is that you can make it in no time, as long as the chickpea stew is prepared a bit in advance and warmed up!

Leblebi:
- Chickpeas, rehydrated and cooked in their liquid until medium soft like the ones you get in a can. Make sure to keep that liquid!
- Bread, crumbled up into little pieces
- One or two eggs
- Garlic
- Onion
- Spices (ideally tabel spice mix, but you can make your own flavorful spice mix and it should work fine. My on the spot spice mix is thyme, paprika, a teeny bit of cardamom, and a teeny bit of coriander seeds. Much like falafel spices actually)
- Herbs, chopped up (ideally parsley, but sage works surprisingly well, too)
- Can of tuna (optional; can be replaced by another cheap canned fish, like herring or sardines. Some people like to put other meats,

like shredded chicken. That would also be delicious and appropriate)
- Capers (optional)
- Bay leaves (optional)
- Olives (optional)
- Harissa paste (optional; if you cannot find this then just make your own smoky hot sauce: char a hot pepper and blend it with a bit of garlic, onion and water. Any spice will work but harissa is definitely the classic method)

Warm up the chickpeas in their liquid. Add a couple of cloves of garlic and bay leaves to the chickpea liquid mix, as well as one onion, minced. Add spices to the mix. Your chickpea stew is now ready. Poach the egg in the chickpea stew, about one minute. Some people just crack the egg directly on top of the leblebi, up to your discretion.

Shred up the bread into tiny little pieces, with your hand. Top it with the chickpea stew, harissa (or other hot sauce, but harissa is really ideal), egg, tuna (optional), capers (optional), olives (optional) and chopped herbs (optional). Be ready to taste almost authentic Tunisian leblebi! Make sure to mix everything well before eating; the hot chickpea stew will cook the egg if you decided not to poach it in the chickpea stew beforehand.

This can be reduced to an extremely cheap meal if necessary: just pour some chickpea stew on top of some shedded bread! When you get sick of that ramen bowl, trust me, if you did a good job spicing up the chickpea stew this will be amazing. Just shredded bread and chickpea stew! What else could you ask for?

**Broccoli with lemon breadcrumbs**
Broccoli is delicious. Lemon broccoli is even better. But broccoli with lemon breadcrumbs? Absolutely incredible. It is so amazing, yet also so simple to make! This is another great recipe to wow someone on a date for cheap: they will have probably never thought of doing this.

Broccoli with lemon breadcrumbs:
- Broccoli
- Lemons + some zest
- Breadcrumbs
- garlic
- Seasoning for the breadcrumbs (salt, pepper a must, onion powder and garlic powder highly recommended, herbs such as thyme parsley basil are great as well. But basically the highlight is the lemon so just salt and pepper on the breadcrumbs should technically be enough)

- Oil

Season the breadcrumbs. mix them with a bit of salt, pepper and other seasonings, if you have. add lemon juice to the breadcrumb mix. This will make the breadcrumbs soft, but cooking the breadcrumbs will get rid of this issue. Add the zest of one lemon as well. Toast the breadcrumbs in a pan, until they are nice and golden
Put the broccoli in the oven, with a bit of salt, pepper, garlic and olive oil. Cook until the tips start to brown slightly, then add the breadcrumbs. Cook for 5 more minutes, season, and serve. This recipe is so good, even broccoli haters will enjoy it!

## Herring with yogurt-apple sauce and mashed potatoes.

Herring has a strong flavor. It is a powerful fish. However, well balanced, Herring is absolutely amazing. The best part about Herring, it is one of the cheapest fishes money can buy, especially in Europe. If you cannot find herring, it is ok as this dish works with most white fishes. Even sardines should work for this recipe.
To make the mashed potatoes: I know that you can start making them from scratch, but that can become incredibly time consuming. Powdered bags of mashed potatoes can taste absolutely fine, and don't require as

much work as if starting from scratch. Also, with these bags, you don't have to use as much butter or milk as traditional mashed potatoes. Finally, these bags are ridiculously cheap and tasty: for one dollar, you can get 4 servings of mashed potatoes! That is absolutely incredible.

Herring with yogurt sauce and mashed potatoes:
- Herring
- Apples
- Yogurt
- Acid (vinegar or lemon juice)
- Herbs (optional; ideally dill but i know that is expensive; most herbs will work)
- Shallots (red onions or white work fine as well, but shallots are preferred)
- Salt, pepper
- Mashed potatoes packet (or homemade mashed potatoes, your choice really)

Make the yogurt sauce: julienne the apples, mince the shallots. Mix them with the yogurt, acid, salt, pepper and herbs (optional). Prepare the mashed potatoes packet, as directed on the packet. Every packet is slightly different proportions of water and mashed potatoes packet.
Take the herring out of the jar (most herrings are pre-cooked and saved in oil), and start plating: mashed

potatoes, then herring, then yogurt sauce. Serve and enjoy.

**Homemade mashed potatoes:** .
Simple staple, it is important to have a recipe of it! Some people remove the skin, some people don't. Depends how silky smooth or rustic of a feel you want your mashed potatoes to have. Since this is dorm room cooking, I highly recommend that you keep the skins on, as it takes less time and prep to make the mashed potatoes + there are many good vitamins and minerals on the potato skins. The recipe

Mashed potatoes:
- Potatoes
- Milk or cream (optional)
- Butter or oil (I recommend butter if you can afford it)
- Salt, pepper, herbs

Cut the larger potatoes into the same size as the smaller ones, so that all are roughly the same size. Boil the potatoes in salted water, for 30-40 minutes or until the potatoes are extremely soft, almost crumbling to the touch. Drain the potatoes, keeping a teeny bit of the potato water, and mash them with a potato masher, or a fork, adding the milk (or cream) and butter (or oil) while you are mashing. Mash until the consistency is as you like it. You can add some of the potato water to make your mashed potatoes thicker or thinner, as you like. Finish with the herbs, salt and pepper. Mashed potatoes go well with almost any dish!

**Quinoa, tuna and celery salad**
Quinoa is ridiculously expensive, I know. But, once in a while, there are sales on quinoa, which can make it even cheaper than pasta. During those moments, it is best to buy some quinoa and start making delicious food with it. This recipe is a perfect example of that.

Quinoa tuna and celery salad:
- Quinoa
- Tuna
- Celery
- Shallots
- Red kidney beans, cooked (canned or dehydrated it doesn't matter as long as they are properly cooked)
- Salt, pepper
- Lemon juice
- Olive oil

Cook the quinoa, making sure that the water is properly salted. mince the celery and shallots, and add them to a large bowl. add the tuna and strained kidney beans to the bowl. add the quinoa, lemon juice, salt and pepper to the bowl as well. don't add too much salt because the tuna and quinoa will already be quite salty. mix everything together, until homogenous, and serve.

**Ice cream and jam**
I had this idea one day when I went to the convenience store at 4am, craving some ice cream. They had this cool korean fish-looking ice cream, which was around 4 dollars. I know that is incredibly expensive but it was sooo worth it. It was an ice cream sandwich with sugar cone as the sandwich bread, with some red bean paste as filling as well. It was so good I thought: why not include something similar in this cookbook? This recipe is so simple I won't even write much about it: simply just mix ice cream with some jam, any kind of jam, and you re in heaven. For a crunchy element you can add crumbled cookies, or even crackers sprinkled with some sugar (and cinnamon if you have) then toasted in the oven work quite amazing on top of ice cream. This proves yet again that crackers can be incredibly versatile!

**Fried bread**
This dish is definitely an end of the month dish, because of how cheap it is. I actually started thinking

about this dish after coming back from China, where fried bread is sold almost everywhere, alongside a bit of condensed milk for sweetness. My recipe is salty, best used for breakfast or snack type dishes, but i will absolutely add condensed milk as an optional ingredient for this recipe. This is best used oon slightly old and crusty bread, because then you are giving the bread a type of second life. Anyways here is the recipe:

Fried bread:
- Bread
- Oil/butter
- Salt
- Condensed milk (optional)

Add the oil (or butter) to a hot pan. fry the bread. cover with a little bit of salt. Finished! add toppings as you would like, the condensed milk being the one most commonly used in China.

**Leftover Omelette recipe**
Picture this scenario: it is Sunday, most farmers markets are closed and the convenience store next door is way too pricey. You check your fridge, and all there is are some eggs along with a couple of random vegetables and sauces. What do you do? why, a leftover omelette of course!

Omelettes, and eggs in general, can really divide the novice cooks from the pros. Sure, it is easy to make an omelette, but a good, creamy, succulent omelette? Skill is needed. I try to give the best tutorial possible in this recipe, in order to succeed right away on the first try.

In terms of leftovers that can be applied into the omelette, I am very liberal about this. Once, I put sriracha, some leftover breadcrumbs and a can of chopped olives, and trust me when I say that this omelette was absolutely delicious. However, I will of course give come classic combinations which go great in any omelette. The recipe:

- Eggs
- Milk (optional; whole milk is ideal but any type of milk will absolutely work)
- Salt, pepper to taste
- Leftovers

Some classic leftover combinations (please, feel free to experiment on this one!) :

- Onions, peppers, hot chilis
- Mushrooms, cheese
- Just onions
- Garlic, shallots
- Pasta
- Leftover pasta (think of all of those delicious carbs!)
- Basil, tomato, mozzarella
- Dill, fish (leftover or not)

- Beans, rice (burrito style heheh)
- Cilantro, garlic, tomato, onion
- Parsley and garlic
- Parmesan, arugula (as a topping)
- Leftover meats
- Leftover chinese food
- Fish sauce, soy sauce, ginger
- And the list goes on and on…..

Crack the eggs in a bowl, and whisk them together. Add all seasonings (salt, soy sauce or other) into this mixture. Add a bit of milk (optional) into this mixture as well.

On a hot pan, heat up the leftover ingredients that you would like to add. Once they are hot and browning, lower the heat and add the egg mixture. stir this egg mixture very carefully, pushing the batter from the sides of the pan toward the center of the pan. cook, on low heat, until cooked to your liking. My ideal omelette is extremely creamy in the middle, with a very soft exterior. once the desired creamy consistency is ready, remove the pan from the heat, and add a teeny bit of milk (optional) in order to stop the cooking process. This also enables a creamier omelette. fold in half, and serve, alongside some sauces and garnishes if desired. All leftover problems, solved with the help of a few eggs.

**Homemade bagel bites**

I came up with this recipe after staying over at a friend's place. Around 2 am we were hungry and he proposed that we eat some bagel bites. I looked at that thing, and thought to myself holy crap this is so easy to make homemade. It will be cheaper and better. That being said, bagel bites at the supermarket are incredibly cheap still, and I highly recommend that you buy a bunch of these if your budget allows it. They will save your life when you really wanna watch that last netflix episode at 4-5am and are way too lazy to cook. Then again, the bagel bites that we are making can also fit in the freezer, so it's anyone's call really if they want to invest in store bought bagel bites or not.

Disclaimer: I know that bagel bites generally have a hole in them. My bagel bites do not necessarily have a hole in them. This is because we are exercising the DRD budget. Whatever can be used as the base, whether it is actual mini bagels or slices of bread or even thinly sliced vegetables, will be used as the base. No matter what, the base is smothered in tomato sauce and cheap cheese, so it will definitely be delicious and eaten within seconds by all of your friends and roommates. The recipe:

homemade bagel bites:

- Bagel base (ideally mini bagels, but we can get creative: chapati or paratha, cooked beforehand, flattened Turkish "fladenbrot" as

they say here in Berlin, baguette, cut lengthwise and flattened ideally in a panini press (although sticking it in the oven with something really heavy on top of it will work just fine), thinly sliced eggplant, grilled or baked until slightly crispy, very thinly sliced zucchini or other large vegetables sliced thinly can also be a base)
- Tomato sauce
- Cheese
- Toppings (some people like tiny pepperoni squares or garlic or something on top of the bagel bites, I personally really like just plain bagel bites. Cheaper too)

Assemble the bagel bites: if needed to toast the base in order to not make it too soggy, do so now. Cover the base with tomato sauce. Another way to try and avoid maximum sogginess is to smother the tomato sauce on already frozen bread, minimizing the sogginess when put back into the freezer.
Add the cheese. Either store in freezer or pop them into the oven immediately. Depending on the size of the bagel bites, leave them in between 5-15 minutes. If they are frozen, add an extra 2-3 minutes cooking time. No matter what, the best way to ensure that the bagel bites are not burning is just to check on them every so often.

And BOOM! Voila! You just made a world-renowned party snack!

**Potato hash with egg**

When living on a budget, you will quickly find out that potatoes are life, and they never go away. Summer, winter, autumn and spring, potatoes are available and cheap. They are almost cheaper than rice. Especially if you have a costco membership, you can get a huge bag of 50lbs of potatoes for less than 20 bucks! That is a lot of potatoes, so be careful to not waste any by waiting too long, like my roommates always did. Basically, you have to eat a lot of potatoes. This egg and potato hash is a great, simple recipe where you can use up some potatoes quickly.

Potato hash with egg:
- Potatoes
- Egg
- Condiments (optional)
- Salt, pepper to taste

Cube the potatoes. You want them to be big, but not too big, so that the hash can have some nice crispy bits.

Blanch the potatoes. Boil them in water for 5-10 minutes, until they are very soft. Then, drain them and stick them in a hot pan with some oil. fry them on medium heat until everything is nice and golden brown. This can take some time: it took me 30-40 minutes once. The mistake most people do is turning the pan on too high, getting the exterior nice and crispy but failing to cook the middle of the potato cubes. Then, add the eggs and cook them to you liking. I like turning off the heat and scrambling my eggs, using just the leftover heat of the pan, ensuring nice and runny scrambled eggs, but to each their own thing.
Serve, with some condiments. A cheap, incredible breakfast is served :)

Side note: if you are really broke, remove the egg! trust me, a potato hash with just potatoes is still delicious :)


**Wtf pasta**
The WTF pasta is very similar to the leftover omelette. You cook pasta, then dump your whole fridge into it. As long as you don't go too crazy, adding chocolate and vanilla extract and such, the resulting pasta will usually turn out to be quite delicious. This is another great manner to use up all of your leftovers. Whenever I was too lazy to cook an

exciting dish, I usually resorted to WTF pasta, due to its simplicity and the fact that it can take either few or many ingredients, up to my discretion. The recipe:

Wtf pasta:
- Pasta (any kind, multiple kinds of pasta work too but just read the cooking times on the packet and make sure to add each pasta at the proper time so that they all are perfectly cooked when it is time to strain the pasta)
- All leftovers. I have once used ketchup, bbq sauce, some leftover meat, and zucchini, and it was actually quite delicious!

Boil a large pot of heavily salted water. Add the pasta, different pastas during different intervals if the cooking times for each type are different. Strain, keeping a small amount of the pasta water at hand in a glass or bowl or something right before you strain the pasta.

Add all leftovers, cooked or not (to your discretion) into the pasta, along with a little bit of pasta water. Mix everything up, and serve. All leftover problems are solved with this one simple yet delicious recipe.

**Bruschetta**

Ahhh, man am I a sucker for bruschetta. It is so simple, yet so incredibly delicious and versatile. It is just toasted bread with some kind of topping. Some people put tomato, mozzarella and basil. Some people put tapenade, which is a type of olive spread. Some people put a dollop of ricotta cheese, along with a teeny bit of liver paste and pine nuts. Possibilities with bruschetta are endless.

The best bread for Bruschetta is of course baguette, but again this is extreme dorm cooking so we have to be extremely flexible with our ingredients. As long as there is toast and something we can spread on top of the toast, screw it, let's call that bruschetta in order to impress all of our friends and guests. Even the strangest breads can be sliced down to something which is flat and can be toasted.

Since bruschetta is so incredibly versatile, I will add my favorite cheap toppings as a recommendation on what to put on top of the bruschetta. However, please do not limit yourself to these insanely powerful combinations: try your own! Maybe you will come up with something even cheaper and more delicious than what I propose…

Bruschetta:
- Bread, with some part flat enough so that we can spread something onto it
- Toppings
- Salt, pepper oil (olive oil or herb oil is best)

Drizzle some salt, pepper and oil onto the bread. toast the bread, until crispy. If the bread is thick enough, having some charred parts on the bread is delicious and will work marvelously with almost all toppings.

If the toasts are very thick and don't fit into the toaster, no problem, just stick them in the oven. When the bread is toasted, smear the toppings on top of the bread, and drizzle with some more oil if you would like. BAM. You just made a fancy dish called bruschetta.

Topping ideas:
- Tomato, garlic, basil, chopped extremely finely
- Artichoke dip
- Hummus with a bit of paprika
- Cheese, any and all cheeses. Classic is ricotta with pine nuts and basil however
- Tuna salad, but no mayo in the tuna salad (could also add mayo if desired, I personally prefer it without for bruschetta)
- Tapenade, which is olives which are pitted and blended with a little seasonings like fresh garlic and some onion powder with capers
- Whole tomatoes and mozzarella (back to the whole bagel bites thing here)
- Canned fish, mixed with some lemon, shallots and herbs like dill
- Red pepper dip
- Beer cheese
- Whatever your mind comes up with; the internet is a great source of inspiration, especially when it comes to bruschetta toppings.

**Hush puppies**

Why are we doing hush puppies? Because they are a southern classic! Produced during the times when people struggled to get food on the plate, these hush puppies are going to be filling and delicious. Furthermore, they are a great American staple, and can be stuffed with almost anything you like: cheese, collard greens, meat, onions, etc; the only limit to the possible fillings in hush puppies is from one's own imagination. Even sweet sugar and cinnamon hush puppies are possible! The recipe:

Hush puppies:
- Cornmeal (ideally that self rising type of cornmeal; you can use any cornmeal but the self rising type is ideal; the hush puppies come out more puffy and airy this way)
- Flour
- One egg
- Buttermilk (any type of milk will work, but buttermilk definitely has a higher fat content and is more ideal for this recipe)
- Pinch of salt
- Sugar
- 1 shredded white onion (optional but highly recommended)

- Fillings (up to your discretion, but as usual I will give some classic combinations)

Mix all of the dry ingredients (salt, sugar, cornmeal, flour, onion) together. Add the milk and the egg, until the formation of a fairly sticky dough.
Heat up a pot of oil. Add your fillings to the dough if desired. Fry the hush puppies by dropping the dough into the oil, one spoonful at a time. Fry until golden brown, about 2 to 3 minutes on each side.
Serve, with a sauce if desired (the spicy remoulade sauce works really well with these hush puppies, that's for sure)
filling ideas:
- Cheese, jalapeno and bacon
- Just cheese
- Collard greens, garlic or/and shallots
- Broccoli, peas, cheese, thyme, bacon
- Thyme
- Rosemary and pepper
- Shrimp
- Beef jerky
- Your imagination!

**Kati roll.**
In principle, a kati roll is pretty simple. It's basically just some fillings wrapped inside a nice naan. There can be vegetarian types of kati rolls, vegan types of

rolls; some can be filled with fish, some with meat. A kati roll is basically nothing more than a glorified sandwich wrap. But, man oh man is it delicious, seriously.

For kati rolls, one is meant to use naan bread. If you own a tandoor, then great! You can make naan bread everyday if you want to. However, most people reading this book will definitely not own a tandoor, or even have access to a tandoor, therefore getting access to naan bread will be tricky. Some people claim that they can make naan from an oven; feel free to try any oven made naan recipe, but the real stuff tastes better.

A better idea, however, is to substitute the naan for some chapati bread (pg 65) when making your kati roll. Sure, the bread is not as delicious, but the kati roll is still absolutely splendid even after substituting the bread. The recipe:

kati roll:
- Naan or chapati bread
- Some kind of sauce as a base (mint and garlic sauces are very famous)
- Vegetable garnishes (salad, tomato, thinly sliced onion, cabbage, cucumber, cilantro, just to name a few. No need to go crazy here, as 2-5 types of vegetables should be enough)
- Cheese (optional, and ideally paneer)

- Main filling (could be fish or meat or tofu or something else, but basically the star of the kati roll)

Take out a chapati or naan, and heat it up in the pan or oven. Then, smother it in sauce (recipe for sauces below). add the vegetable garnishes, the main filling, then the cheese. Roll up the kati roll, as you would a burrito. If you have a panini press, now is the perfect time to use it. If you do not own a panini press, no problem, just stick the roll in a hot oven for a couple of minutes, or heat the roll up in a hot pan, making sure that every side of the roll is nice and crispy. Serve, with extra cheese and sauces if you would like. Voila! not more complicated than a sandwich, yet very intense in flavor.

Sauces:

Use a food processor, ideally, because without one these sauces can definitely take a while to whisk before being properly blended:

- Garlic sauce: garlic, salt, lemon juice, neutral oil (like sunflower seed oil or canola oil). Blitz the garlic with the salt a couple of times, scraping down the sides of the food processor bowl each time it gets blitzed. add the neutral oil while the food processor is running, a little bit at a time, and alternate every so often with a bit of lemon juice. Congrats! if the garlic sauce has a mayonnaise-like consistency, then your sauce is a huge success!

- Mint sauce: mint, coriander seeds, a bit of chili, garlic, oil, lemon juice. blend. delicious tahini sauce

Classic fillings:
- Chicken tikka masala
- Lentils in curry
- Fish curry
- Paneer tikka masala
- Vegetarian ball fritters
- Grilled vegetables
- Fried chicken
- Bean fritters
- Falafel
- Your imagination

## Fried veggies with broken bread (the Turkish flatbread fried bread dish)

This recipe is a fun one, because it is basically a vegetable medley mixed with some nice bits of crunchy bread scattered around the dish. The difference in texture makes this dish incredible, and it can be quite filling as well.

When making this dish, remember that most vegetables can be replaced with other vegetables. Just mix up a couple of vegetables, and the dish will probably turn out good. Another reminder that cooking is not an exact science, any bread for this dish will work. I made it with Turkish fladenbrot (a staple in Germany), but feel free to experiment with as many different breads as you would like!

Fried veggies with broken bread:
- Onions
- Hard Veggies (honestly, almost any work. I have tried zucchini, mushrooms, kohlrabi, leeks, carrots, broccoli, apples (not a veggie but why not), turnip and more!)
- Bread
- Oil
- Herbs and seasonings (any you want. No need to go crazy here, one or two is enough. I liked using Paprika and Parsley with garlic powder for the version I made)

Chop up the onions and hard veggies, and saute them in a hot pan with some oil. Once they are properly browned, add some pieces of bread to the dish, as well as herbs and seasonings. Continue to saute. The bread will soak up all of the moisture and flavor in the pan, as well as get slightly toasted. You can finish this dish in the oven, if you like.

Overall, this dish is very similar to a stuffing that you can find during Thanksgiving, if you add nuts and dried cranberries to the dish. However, this is cheap dorm cooking so I thought that this recipe would have more of a use for people than a turkey stuffing recipe.

**Sardines, rice and maggi cubes (robert dish)**

My good friend Robert in Berlin taught me how to make this dish. once, he came home with just sardines and rice, took some items from our kitchen, and made this dish. We all had an exhausting day and did not feel like cooking at all, so he whipped this up in only a couple of minutes and it was absolutely delicious. Cooked rice can take a while, but that's why it may be smart to invest in a rice cooker, in order to always have cooked rice in one's home. Feel free to replace the rice with couscous, as it also works incredibly well! The recipe:
Simple rice salad:
- Sardines, with the oil from the tin
- One or two maggi cubes (a flavoring cube; stock or consomme work fine as well)
- Onions
- Peppers (optional)
- Spice (optional)
- Rice, cooked (or couscous, cooked)

- Lime

Mince the onion and pepper (optional). add it to the cooked rice, along with the sardines, crushed up maggi cube, and sardine oil. finish with lime. season with spice, if you like spicy. No matter what, this dish is absolutely delicious :) great for cheap midnight munchies!

## DESSERT

**Crumble**

Crumbles are fun because they are versatile, and incredibly cheap to make. Now, I know butter is expensive so I sometimes just use ingredients which already have a lot of butter with them, to replace butter. Cakes and cookies fall in this category, and are great for a crumble. Trust me, in college it is easy to get your hands on a lot of cake and/or cookies for free on certain days. It is also possible to create a crumble with vegetable oil (or margarine or whatever, which is necessary to keep from mixing from milk and meat at dessert time if you are keeping kosher), but butter is always preferred for crumbles. Same goes for flour here: I have made incredible crumbles using old cookies and stale cakes, replaced part of the flour with some wet bread, etc. Basically the most important part of the crumble is making sure that the top is crunchy, sweet and flavorful, and there are a million ways to get that amazing texture and flavor. As with many recipes in this book, I am giving the basics, allowing room for creativity.

Crumble:
- Fruit. Any fruit will work but I recommend apple, pear, or even pineapple. Banana works but is a bit soft for a crumble. Nonetheless absolutely delicious!
- Butter (or margarine, or oil)
- Sugar (or mix of sugar and honey)
- Flour (or mix of flour and oats, or crumbled up crackers, cake, etc. Ideally in a blender or something. Basically something to get a nice crust for your crumble. I call this crumbly stuff)
- Mint (optional)
- Pinch of salt

Chop up the fruit and butter a deep dish pan used for baking. A small cake pan will do the trick just fine. Cover the fruit with some sugar and add it to the pan. Mix the butter with the flour/crumbly stuff, until you have some nice crumbly balls. Mix this doughy stuff with some sugar, and add it on top of the fruit. Drizzle with some honey on top, if you like.
Bake in the oven. Done!

## Caramelized apples with whipped cream

It turns out, especially for French dishes, less is definitely more. Instead of buying the whipped cream can, just whip your own cream! That way you can adjust the amount of sugar you would like, as well as the flavoring in the cream. Make sure that the apples you are using are suited for cooking: it would be a shame to have an apple meant for salad (like a nice granny smith, amazing in salad with some herbs and nuts and even green salads) be used in a caramelized "flambe" setting. Then again, apples are apples, and when living on the line anything is possible and any apple will do the job.

I would suggest that you use apples which are especially ripe, so the last apples in the basket, for caramelized apples. The extra ripeness will extract more flavor out of the apples, especially once you mix it with the butter, sugar, touch of salt and vanilla (if available). You can also add white wine or even some alcohol like Rum or Whiskey to the dish, and "Flambe" the dish away to perfection. Don't cook too long, or the apples will get mushy! If this does happen, make a crumble: mix sugar, flour (or unseasoned breadcrumbs) and butter with a touch of salt, stick the "overcooked" apples on a tray, and put the crumble on top. You can flavor the crumble with a touch of mint and/or basil, but that mint should be topped at the end in my opinion. You can also make a mint and/or basil whipped cream, which I find absolutely fabulous

For the caramelized apples:
- Apples (or most fruits, honestly. Melon and pineapple are great as well!)
- Butter
- Sugar
- Touch of salt
- Vanilla (optional, can also use vanilla sugar which is very nice as well)
- Booze (ideally a vanilla-like flavored booze. I tried Fireball once, and the cinnamon really came through into the dish!)
- Basil or mint (optional)

Melt butter in pan. Stick the apples in and cook for 2-3 minutes. Add sugar, salt, vanilla, and booze. "Flambe" the booze away, until the fire fades away. Now, it is ready! Serve it with some chopped herbs on top (optional) and, of course, the amazing homemade whipped cream.

For the whipped cream:
- Heavy whipping cream
- Sugar (about 1-3 tbsp, depends how sweet you want it)

- Herbs (optional, mint or basil recommended. Nutmeg is very nice as well, and some people like cinnamon. Vanilla flavoring is the classic one)

Whip the cream into oblivion, adding sugar halfway through and herbs around the end. Be careful not to over-whip or the cream will turn into butter! The ideal time to stop is when little peaks start happening on your whipped cream when removing the whisk. This can be a 10 minute effort, or even longer, especially if you are using a fork, so be patient! It is definitely worth the effort in my opinion.

**Minty fruit salad soup**
This salad is great, because it will combine a lot of fruits that are about to go bad. The fruit salad will taste good for 2-3 days, so it is a great way to eat your leftover fruits at the end of the week. Buying a lot in bulk to save money means also using a lot, so this is definitely a dish to share with the roommates or even the entire floor, everyone will be extremely grateful later on for sure!
Basically, the way to make this fruit salad is to prepare this amazing mint soup, and then adding a lot of chopped fruits inside. Make sure that the fruits that you are adding make sense with each other: I will give example of tried and true combinations that work in my opinion. But, in all honesty a fruit salad is a

fruit salad, almost all combinations of fruits are possible and delicious.

For the minty soup:
- Mint (and basil, optionally)
- Water
- Sugar
- White wine (optional but very recommended)
- Pinch of salt
- Lemon juice (optional)

Boil water. Add sugar and white wine, then cook down for about 3 minutes. Turn off the heat, and put the mint, whole, into the water. Then, cover and stick in the fridge, until the syrupy soup is cold

While waiting, chop up your fruits. Once the soup is cold, remove from fridge and stick chopped fruits inside. You can add a bit of lemon juice into the final mixture if you like, some people like that. Some people also like to add some booze like rum, as a final touch, but that is all up to you.

Simple fruit combination ideas:
- Strawberries, raspberries, cantaloupe, grapes, blueberries
- Grapes, watermelon, cantaloupe, bananas, apples
- Apples, pears, grapes

- Mango, litchi, apple (lemongrass can be nice as well)

But the best advice I can give for this is when you are at the cheap farmer's market, check what is in season, ask the farmers what they think is incredible and cheap, and ask them what a great fruit salad would be. That fruit salad will most likely work with the mint soup I described.

If it is winter and honestly very few fruits are in season, then definitely do not over-complicate it! Sometimes just one or two fruits is enough, so don't worry about it!


**Rice milk**

This recipe is honestly one of the quickest desserts one can make, as long as the rice was cooked in advance. Again, a huge thanks to Robert for introducing this incredibly quick recipe to me. It is a great way to use leftover rice. Leftover couscous also works extremely well for this recipe. The secret to making this dish perfect is to make sure that the proportions are correct: too much milk, and it's too soupey. Too much condensed milk, it will be too sweet. No matter what, this is one of the cheaper desserts money can make, so it is definitely worth trying. Experiment with different flavors, until you find your favorite rice milk! My favorite flavor is added a teeny bit of nutmeg and cinnamon at the end

:) I sprinkle it right on top of the bowl before serving, to make the food a little prettier than just rice and milk.

Rice milk:
- Rice, cooked and cooled down (couscous also works, any starch really. My friend Robert even did it with bread once. But rice or couscous are ideal in my opinion)
- Milk
- Yogurt
- Condensed milk
- Teeny bit of salt
- Seasonings/flavorings (optional)


Mix all ingredients together in large bowl, adding the seasonings/flavorings at the end. Place in fridge for a couple of hours, until the rice milk is cold. Boom! You just created rice milk! Some people bake this, in order to create rice pudding, but I actually really enjoy the consistency of rice milk a bit more than rice pudding. Seasonings ideas:
- Chocolate syrup and/or maple syrup
- Basil with nutmeg
- Cinnamon
- Pepper
- Ground chili

Many seasonings will work, but just be careful and avoid anything sour, as adding that that will make the milk curd and completely destroy the rice milk. Almost any other seasoning will work fine, however!

**Chocolate mousse**

Another great way to impress your friends and make them believe that you are the fanciest person alive! In reality, chocolate mousse is just eggs and chocolate. Any chocolate will work. Adding some vanilla is a recommended option, as it adds flavor, but it is not absolutely necessary either. To be extra fancy, add some shaved chocolate on top, or cocoa powder. Some people add candied orange peels or whipped cream, but in my opinion simplicity is key. The recipe:

Chocolate mousse:
- Chocolate
- Egg
- Pinch of salt
- Decorations ( already mentioned that chocolate shavings and cocoa powder are great decoration, but feel free to come up with your own!)


Separate the egg yolks from the egg whites. Melt the chocolate, and add the egg yolks once it is off of the heat. We don't want the egg yolks to cook. In a separate bowl, beat the egg whites with a pinch of salt until they form white peaks. Fold the beaten egg whites to the chocolate mixture. Fill this airy chocolate mixture into some containers, and let it cool down for at least 2 hours in the fridge. Finish with some decorations, before serving your delicious creation. Now, everyone in the house will definitely think that you are a professional chef, once you make chocolate mousse!

**The Dorm Room Delights cake template**

Whenever there is a birthday party, there is a cake. And that cake can cost quite a bit of money if you buy it at the store! More importantly, your friends will be thinking that your homemade cake is filled with more love than any store bought cake. This cake can cost the fraction of the price of a store bought cake. Even if our cake does not come out perfect, there is always a way to salvage it with some delicious icing, making the overall experience absolutely delicious.
I call this the cake template, because without these main ingredients it will be tough to bake a cake. But you can definitely add elements to the cake. Once I added yogurt and lime, the cake still worked and was absolutely delicious :) The trick to a delicious cake is

making sure that the batter is nice and airy, in order to ensure a super moist cake at the end :)

DRD cake template:
- Eggs
- Flour
- Butter
- Sugar
- Baking powder
- Seasonings
- Pinch of salt
- Vanilla, orange essence or rosewater (optional)

Indeed, my ideal basis for cake is a pound cake. It is just so rich and moist… but to this pound cake you can add an almost unlimited amount of seasonings and ingredients, allowing you to make many other types of cakes and flavors just based on this simple template. If adding chocolate or other sweet ingredients, then no need to add as much sugar to the dish, remember!
So, a pound cake is: a quarter eggs, a quarter flour, a quarter butter, a quarter sugar. If measurements are off a couple of grams, don't worry, the cake will still be most likely fine and just as delicious.

Cream the butter and sugar, until they become one. Separate the egg whites from the yolks. Add the egg yolks, baking powder, vanilla (optional) and flour to the cake batter. In a separate bowl, beat the egg whites with a pinch of salt, until they form white peaks. Fold in the egg whites with the cake batter. Bake the cake in a buttered ( or oiled, or buttered and sugared or floured) pan, at 200C for about 15-20 minutes. Check if it's ready by inserting a toothpick into the cake. If it comes out dry and not full of sticky batter, then the cake is ready. Cool and unmold the cake. Ice the cake. Finished!

To this template batter, thousands of different combinations and fillings can be created. You can add lemon zest, poppy seeds and lemon juice to make lemon poppy seed cake. You can add melted chocolate to make chocolate cake. You can add lemon peels, sage, and thyme if you would like. You can make a yogurt cake. You can add nuts and chocolate chips to that yogurt cake. You can make banana bread. You can make cinnamon cake. You can make rum cake. Confetti cake. So many possibilities, it's incredible! Just add the ingredient before folding the egg whites into the cake. Depending on what you add, you may need to slightly change the amount of egg, sugar, flour or butter in the recipe, but no worries even if you don't the cake will most likely still be fine, as long as ridiculous quantities of fillings are not being added to the batter. Just focus on getting the nicest, airiest batter possible for best cake moistness. Make sure to ice the cake!

Cake icing:
- Powdered sugar
- Any type of liquid. Orange juice, coffee, olive oil, melted chocolate, melted butter, rosewater, etc. will all work and give a hint of different flavors, but just plain water will work fine as well. You only need a small amount of liquid compared to powdered sugar, so add it slowly and with caution!

Mix the powdered sugar with the liquid, until a icing-like consistency has been formed. You will notice that lots of powdered sugar is needed for only a bit of liquid. Some people like very thick icings, some people like almost watery icings (like the one found on donuts). Your choice to decide how thick you want your icing to be. Once the icing is of the thickness and consistency that you are happy with, then the icing is ready to be put on the cake. For buttercream icing, the proportions are half butter half powdered sugar, just make sure that the butter is neither too warm nor too cold for an easy incorporation of the butter to the sugar.

After the cake is iced, it is officially ready to get the candles and get that birthday party started! Have your friends pitch in for the cake, and trust me that making the cake yourself will be the cheapest and tastiest option for a birthday party.

## EPILOGUE

I have just shared with you all of the recipes and tricks that I have used throughout college to stay full and healthy! Please, feel free to take a picture of your wildest creations and tag me on Instragram, @rex_in_thecity. You might even get lucky, and I could provide some feedback about your dish! Also, let me know which crazy creations you managed to come up with thanks to the recipe templates in this book! I am always here for advice, so feel free to message me :)

**Biography of Rex Elardo**

Born in Utah, grew up in Paris, went to college in Boston at Northeastern University, Rex Elardo always had a passion for travel and food. He developed his love for cooking after being thrust into baking bread during a class trip at the age of 10. His mom gifted him a pancake flipper and soon enough his career in the kitchen began to flourish. Taking his passion into the world of fine dining, Rex interned at

Apicius, a 2-star Michelin restaurant, at the age of 16. He returned to the United States in 2013 to study Industrial Engineering at Northeastern University in Boston. However, his culinary journey did not end there. Rex worked at ACME in New York City over the summer of his first undergraduate year and followed by working at Feast the following summer, both located in the trendy East Village of Manhattan.

After these enriching experiences in upscale dining, Rex turned towards restaurant management, assuming the position of assistant manager at the Rice Barn, a popular Thai eatery in Needham, Massachusetts. Dig Inn, a rapidly-growing chain of locally-sourced restaurants, recruited Rex as a 'garde manger'. A firm believer in diversifying one's knowledge of the different inputs towards the perfect meal, Rex worked part-time with a local catering company and was hand picked to be a cook in a popular Boston-based food truck, Moyzilla, serving Asian street food and dumplings. At the ripe age of 21, Rex was already endowed with working in different types of establishments, assuming all possible positions inside and outside of the kitchen, and serving vastly different patrons a variety of international cuisines. He even made sure to get experience as a bartender while taking his final classes prior to his graduation in 2018 — all while simultaneously working at two other Boston establishments!

During his time in Boston, he realized that many college students struggle to feed themselves in a delicious and healthy manner for cheap. He saw so much food going to waste, and wanted to educate students on how simple it is to maintain a delicious, simple and healthy diet while still in college and not having much time to cook. He never spent more than 20 dollars a week on food, saving up all of the money he made to fund countless adventures, from Haiti to Cancun to Dominican republic to Montreal and more. He even went to Lexington, Kentucky once, for the sole purpose of trying Pappy van Winkle Bourbon (visiting some friends along the way)! With his expertise, he is confident his readers will embrace the kitchen.

Made in the USA
Monee, IL
30 June 2020